FOOD FOR THE THINKING MIND

K SRI DHAMMANANDA

Publication of the

Buddhist Missionary Society Malaysia
Buddhist Maha Vihara,
123, Jalan Berhala,
50470 Kuala Lumpur, Malaysia

Malaysian First Edition 1999

Perpustakaan Negara Malaysia
Cataloguing-in-Publication Data
Dhammananda, K. Sri, 1919-
Food for the Thinking Mind -
K. Sri Dhammananda.
ISBN 967-9920-78-X
1. Religion-Quotations, maxims, etc.
2. Man (Theology) -
Quotations, maxims, etc.
I. Title.
082

1st printing: 12,500 copies (March 1999)
2nd printing: 4,000 copies (April 1999)

Reprinted for free distribution by

Printed and donated for free distribution by
The Corporate Body of the Buddha Educational Foundation
11F., 55 Hang Chow South Road Sec 1, Taipei, Taiwan, R.O.C.
Tel: 886-2-23951198 , Fax: 886-2-23913415
Email: overseas@budaedu.org
Website:http://www.budaedu.org

Contents

Contents

Foreword

s the title suggests, this book is not directed at readers with a particular religious affiliation but is meant for anyone who wishes to reflect on what famous thinkers throughout the ages have written about the human condition. No one can deny that despite temporary flashes of happiness, on the whole, the human condition is far from satisfactory. Human beings have always dreamed of attaining perfect happiness by transcending human problems, generally without much success. However some great thinkers, widely separated in time and space have pondered over how this human condition can be understood and how happiness can be attained. They were able to crystallise these thoughts into clear, apt sayings which sound simple at first sight, but which draw deep from the well springs of human experience. This book is a collection of these thoughts and readers are invited to share them and benefit from them. By reflection, the reader gains an understanding of his or her condition and is thus enabled to live a happier more meaningful life. Most of our problems arise from the fact that we do not understand the cause of our feelings of discontent and unsatisfactoriness.

Human beings are creatures driven by desires. They are constantly seeking to gratify the various demands made by their six senses: smell, hearing, taste, touch, sight and mind. In Buddhism these needs are classified, under four categories. It is stated that the human beings need four kinds of sustenance to satisfy:

- The body
- The senses
- The mind
- The consciousness

As can be readily perceived, the satisfaction of the demands made by the body and the senses are considered coarse and base because even animals have these needs. The satisfaction of the demands made by the mind caters for our natural curiosity about the world around us. This knowledge is then utilised by science and technology to make life more comfortable for us in a physical sense but creature comforts cannot give us ultimate happiness because they do not satisfy our 'self-actualisation' needs.

To find meaning in our existence and to transcend the human condition, we need answers to the great existential questions: Who am I? What am I doing here? Am I needed? However, simply giving academic answers to those questions cannot give a person lasting happiness.

Happiness can only be gained by completely purifying one's consciousness and removing the defilements of restlessness, doubt and worry. Empirical knowledge of the world can be used to help one prepare for the real task of 'cooling down the fires of restlessness' which are the root cause of our sufferings.

This book therefore has two functions:

- To provide an enjoyable means to obtain knowledge about the human condition as perceived by the world's great thinkers and
- To encourage the reader to embark on a journey to purify the consciousness and

thereby achieve ultimate and lasting happiness.

The quotations in this book are the sayings of the founders of several religions and also different religious teachers as well as great philosophers, thinkers, scientists, historians, psychologists, politicians, free thinkers and some other publications, too. Their names and references are given in many places. There are many other sayings in this book where references are not given. Most of them are extracted from the books written by the compiler of this book. Each chapter is preceded by comments representing the thoughts of the compiler on the subject.

"Food for the Thinking Mind" is to be treated as a handy reference book to be read over and over again. It can be read when one has a few moments to spare, or just before retiring to bed. It is meant to sharpen one's understanding of the human condition, to make one think clearly about issues such as honest success, wealth, happiness, sorrow, birth, and death. However it is only the 'food'. It cannot be left on a plate. It has to be taken by one in small amounts and digested properly to give strength and vitality to the spirit.

The insights to understand life's imponderables cannot be obtained at one attempt. One has to constantly strive to reach that understanding by returning to the problem over and over again until wisdom arises. Like food; we need it constantly to sustain ourselves, which is why the book is entitled:

"Food for the Thinking Mind"

I wish you a hearty appetite!

Ven. Dr. K. Sri Dhammananda, J.S.M., Ph.D., D. Litt.
Buddhist Maha Vihara,
Kuala Lumpur, Malaysia
14th March 1999

Acknowledgement

It is with great pleasure and gratitude that we acknowledge the selfless and invaluable services of the following persons who gave their full support and assistance in the compilation of this book:-

Ven. Dr. K Anuruddha, Messrs. H. M. A. de Silva, Quah Swee Kheng, Vijaya Samara Wickrama and Dr. Victor Wee for supplying materials and helping in editorial work.

Sister Subodhi, Bobby Sai and Nimala Sai for handling the entire computer work.

Datin Khor Chin Poey, Teng Swee Ai, Sumana Sing, Janet Teoh, Ang Choo Hong, Boon Kok Chee, Lum Chee Yuen, Linda Lum, Yeoh Gaik It, Eddy Yu Chen Lim and Ong Ah Hock for proof reading and also to Chong Hong Choo for supervision of the entire project, layout and design of the book cover.

HUMANITY

Long ago man had seen himself as being in the centre of the Universe, as its most important inhabitant. According to this point of view, the world was made for humans, for themselves to obtain from it what they wanted because they were the most favoured creatures on it and everything that existed on this planet was for their sole pleasure.

This so called 'Humanistic' view may be directly responsible for the terrible rape of our planet and our total disregard for the rights of other beings which co-exist with us. For example, there have been tragic cases where certain species of animals became extinct through needless slaughter by unsympathetic humans in pursuit of their sporting pleasure or business purposes. Even today the subjugation of nature by science and technology is being applauded. We must increase the number of those amongst us who have already realised the vast destruction that has been wrecked by the man in the name of 'progress'. Up until now nature has been most forgiving and it has allowed man to continue to think that this planet was made for him to rape and plunder at will, to satisfy his insatiable greed for material possessions and sensual gratification. Today there are many warning signs to indicate that the comfortable times are about to end. Hopefully, if compassion and Right View will not save the world, then at least the same selfishness and desire for self-preservation and self-gratification will force man to give some sensible thought to our impoverished environment and our suffering fellow-creatures on this earth.

To understand the place of man in the universe from a Buddhist point of view, we must first of all look at the Buddha's views on the cosmos. According to him, the Universe is to be understood in terms of a vast cosmic space. His teaching categorised the whole universe into three groups: planets with living beings, planets with elements and space itself.

We can see man as a specially favoured creature that had come into existence to enjoy the pleasures of a specially formed planet at the centre of the universe. Buddhism views man as tiny beings not only in strength but also in life span. Man is no more than just another creature but with intelligence that inhabits the universe.

Biologically, humans are weaker than any other beings big or small. Other animals are born armed with some sort of weapon for their own protection and survival. Humans, on the other hand, have their minds for everything but not as a weapon. Humans are regarded as cultured living beings because they are to harmonise with others but not to destroy them. Religion was discovered by them for this purpose. Every thing that lives share the same times force which energizes man. They are part of the same cosmic energy which takes various forms during endless rebirths , passing from human to animal , to divine form and back again, motivated by the powerful craving for existence (the survival instinct) which takes them from birth to death and to rebirth again in a never-ending cycle called samsara. The three detrimental sources of man which bind him to samsara are Greed, Hatred and Delusion.

This cycle can only be broken irrevocably through the development of Wisdom which destroys these fetters and puts an end to craving. Our shared fate as beings who inhabit this planet is that we all want desperately to go on living.

All things depend on each other for their existence. A man cannot see himself as different from (let alone being superior to) other beings because his body is solely dependent on food, which means he is dependent on plants, water, oxygen, etc. for his existence. At the same time his mind also exits dependently because the existence of thoughts rely on sense data which are derived from the external world of objects and persons. The whole universe must be seen as an immensenet: if only one knot in it is shaken, the whole net vibrates. Man owes allegiance to the world because he is dependent on it for his existence both physically and mentally.

1

Nature of the Mind

odern discoveries are confirming what the Buddha had realised twenty-five centuries ago: that the mind is not a thing or an entity with a separate existence but that, which arises dependent on conditions.

It is an energetic intelligent force, which arises in an individual and which can be cultivated to develop positive values such as kindness, sympathy, compassion, and love. These values can be utilised to serve the world. A powerful mind, fully developed, like that of a Buddha's can even purify the atmosphere. On the other hand, when abused by developing negative qualities like hatred, greed, jealousy, and ill-will it can become a potent destructive force. A mind like Hitler's, Idi Amin's, or Pol Pot's can be a source of great misery and suffering to living beings. On a smaller scale, individual humans can also create sufferings to those around them. A mind, which is not properly guarded and trained, can become a dangerous force.

In modern times, great minds are being exerted to discover many truths about the workings of the universe through science. But if these discoveries are allowed to be used by untrained minds, great havoc can result. We only have to consider how the discovery of nuclear fission led to the creation of the most horrible weapons of destruction in our own time. The human mind is capable of great achievements that benefit all human beings, but conversely, it can also be the source of untold sufferings. In trying to explain the tremendous power of the mind, Einstein had said, "Science may have split the atom but it cannot control the mind." What he meant was that mental energy was far more powerful than atomic energy.

The only way this tremendous energy can be harnessed and controlled, is by adopting the age-old mind controlling techniques developed by the ancient sages of the past, like the Buddha. In his teachings, the Buddha analysed the workings of the human mind, its function and its development. He then showed how, given proper spiritual guidance, the mind can be directed to work for the benefit of all living things.

The nature of the mind

The mind is naturally radiant,
But external objects pollute the mind
Through the influence of the senses
And mental faculties of defilement.

~ Buddha - A. I: 10 ~

Use the mind with reasoning

As a man with good eyesight,
on a journey,
Would endeavour to avoid any dangerous place,
So too a wise man in the world of the living
Should avoid demeritorious deeds.

~ Buddha ~

Mind becomes stronger through difficulties

Difficulties strengthen the mind,
as labour does the body.

Human mind and problems

No problem of human destiny
is beyond the reach of man.

~ John Kennedy ~

Nature of the mind changes the world

Besides man-made disasters, some other forms of natural disasters also occur due to human mental pollution. It is mentioned in the teachings of the Buddha, that man's immoral way of life and his mental pollutions, such as hatred, cruelty, jealousy and impatience cause natural disasters. On the other hand, when radiating compassion and mental purity, love and sympathy develop in the mind.

The natural law of cosmic energy functions smoothly. So we can change the world by controlling the mind.

The word of truth

All mental states have mind as their forerunner,
Mind is their chief, and they are mind-made.
If one speaks or acts, with a defiled mind,
Suffering follows one even as the wheel follows the hoof of the draught ox.

~ Buddha - Dh. 1~

No world without mind

By mind the world is led,
By mind the world is moved.
And all good and bad things
Exist in the world because of mind.

~ Buddha - S. I: 39 ~

Thoughts create our destiny

Thoughts are the invisible
builders of our destiny.
Mind is like the ocean and
thoughts are like waves.

Wrongly directed mind can do more harm

Whatever an enemy might do to an opponent,
Or a hater to those he hates,
A wrongly directed mind
Can do even greater harm than that.

~ Buddha ~

Nature of the Mind

Mind runs faster than anything else does

I consider, monks, that there is no phenomenon
That comes and goes so quickly as the mind.
It is not easy to find a simile to show
How quickly mind comes and goes.

~ Buddha ~

The right mental attitude

Be like a lion that trembles not at sounds.
Be like the wind that does not
Cling to the meshes of a net.
Be like a lotus that is not contaminated
By the mud from which it springs up.
Wander alone like a rhinoceros.

~ Buddha - Sn: 71 ~

Man must be open-minded

Mindfulness makes a full man. A full man speaks with an open mind. And like a parachute, the mind works better when it is fully opened.

This awareness is the key to unlock the door from which conflict and strife as well as wholesome thought emerges.

Train the mind properly

When this mind is properly trained, the purpose of life can be experienced. Otherwise, life will be in danger.

We should not follow 'the law of the jungle' by using physical strength, but by using the human mind with a sense of reasoning.

Who does not live even for himself?

He, who does not live in some degree for others, hardly lives for himself.

No suffering when the mind is calm

Whose mind stands like a mountain?
Steady, is not perturbed,
Unattached to things that arouse attachment,
Uninjured by things that provoke anger.
When his mind is cultivated thus,
How can suffering come to him?
Diligent, devoted to the higher mind.
A sage trained in wisdom's ways,
There are no sorrows for the stable one
Who is calm and ever mindful.

~ Buddha ~

Nature of the Mind

Why mindfulness?

Mindfulness, O monks, I declare,
Is essential to all things everywhere.
It is as salt to curry.
Mindfulness, verily, brings great profit.

~ Buddha - A. I: 3 ~

Adjust the mind accordingly

One who does not know how to adjust his mind according to circumstances would be like a corpse in a coffin.

You are your own enemy

No external enemy can harm one as much as one's own thoughts of craving, hate, jealousy and so on.

Tranquillity is never gained from outside

When we are unable to find tranquillity within ourselves, it is useless to seek it elsewhere.

~ La Rochefoucauld ~

We are more concerned with our pain than that of others

The least pain in our little finger gives us more concern and uneasiness than the destruction of millions of our fellow beings.

Calmness creates mental and physical health

A calm and peaceful state of mind is conducive to both mental and physical well being.

~ Bhikkhu Visuddhacara ~

Craving creates suffering

From craving springs grief, from craving springs fear; for him who is wholly free from craving there is no grief, much less fear.

~ Buddha - Dh. ~

Gold and rubbish

Mind is a gold mine and a rubbish heap as well.

Nature of the Mind

Mental attitude not yet changed

There has been outward progress from bullock cart to jet plane but mentally, the individual has not changed at all.

An undeveloped mind

As rain penetrates into an ill-thatched house
So lust penetrates into an undeveloped mind.

~ Buddha - A. I: 9 ~

No suffering when mind is firm

My mind is firm like a rock,
Unattached to sensual things,
Not shaking in the midst
Of a world where all are shaking.
My mind has thus been well developed,
So how can suffering come my way?

~ Th. I: 192 ~

Man is between heaven and hell

Human life lies between heaven and hell because the human mind can be developed easily to experience heavenly bliss and when it is abused, it could very easily experience suffering in hell.

Human robot

Feelings of humanity are fading away from man's mind and in time to come, his behaviour will not be much different from that of a robot. Later, robots may act to replace man.

Atomic energy cannot change the human mind

Atomic energy has shaken and changed the whole world; but even that powerful atomic energy cannot change man's mind. It is still as crooked, unreliable and dangerous as it has been from earliest times. But religion can change man's mind for a better purpose if he really upholds the religious principles.

Nature of the Mind

We are now at the Age of Thought

We have lived through the Stone Age, the Iron Age, the Copper Age, the Religious Fanatic Age, the Scientific Research Age, the Industrial Age and we enter, now, the Age of Thought.

~ Napoleon Hill ~

Madness in everybody

The symptoms of madness can be found in all worldly beings.

~ A Buddhist saying ~

One who has no faith in himself is doomed

Man may have faith in every god,
yet if he has no faith in himself, he is doomed.

~ Swami Vivekananda ~

Uncontrollable thoughts

Thoughts must be properly guided by reason; otherwise, when they burst into action the thinker himself is thereafter powerless to control them.

The tricky nature of the human mind

There were two monks who were living in a temple. Suddenly, one monk started to talk nonsense. The other monk, knowing something was wrong with him and took him to a doctor. He then told the doctor, "Doctor, could you please attend to this monk because I believe that something is wrong with his mind?" Then, the other monk said, "Doctor, actually I am the one who brought him here for treatment. Now, he says that I am the one who needs treatment."

The doctor was confused and could not understand who really needed the treatment. This shows how the human mind can be twisted!

What mind needs?

Neither health nor honour, wealth or power,
Can give the mind a cheerful hour.
When health is lost, be timely wise,
With health all taste of pleasure flies.

Nature of the Mind

Nature of the free mind

Stone walls do not a prison make
Nor iron bars a cage,
A free and quiet mind can take
These for a hermitage.

~ Richard Lovelace ~

The law of vibration and attraction

Any idea that is held in the mind that is either feared or revered will begin at once to clothe itself in the most convenient and appropriate physical forms available.

~ Andrew Carnegie ~

Mind and umbrella

The human mind is like an umbrella –
functions best when open.

~ Walter Gropins ~

Basic law of the mind

As you See — so you feel. As you Feel — so you think. As you Think — so you will. As you Will — so you act.

Thoughts affect the brain

Each thought and feeling is accompanied by a shower of brain chemicals that affect and are affected by billions of cells.

~ Paul Pearsa ~

Master and slave of mind

A wise man will be the master of his mind.
A fool will be its slave.

~ Publius Syrus ~

A calm attitude at all times shows a man of culture

Calmness is not weakness.
A calm attitude at all times shows a man of culture.
It is not difficult for one to be calm
when things are favourable,
But to be composed
when things go wrong is hard indeed.
It is this difficult quality that is worth achieving,
For by exercising such calm and control,
a man builds strength of character.

Nature of the Mind

One mind many hands

A successful team is a group of many hands
but of one mind.

~ Bill Bethel ~

Good and bad

There is nothing either good or bad,
but thinking makes it so.

~ Shakespeare ~

Praise soothes the mind

Praise is so pleasing to the mind of man,
That it is the original motive of
almost all our actions.

~ D. Samuel Johnson ~

Delusion misleads us

No other single thing exists
Like the hindrance of delusion,
Which so obstructs humankind
And makes it wander on forever.

~ Buddha ~

What is meditation?

Meditation is not a way of making your mind quiet. It's a way of entering into the quiet that is already there — buried under the 50,000 thoughts the average person thinks every day.

Mind and body

A human being is a mind with a body,
not a body with a mind.

Man's and animal's nature are in the mind

Instead of saying that man becomes an animal, or an animal becomes man, it would be more correct to say that the karmic force, which manifests in the form of man, may manifest itself in the form of an animal.

The animal nature in the man's mind and human behaviour in the animal's mind are the causes of those occurrences.

Hope leads the way

Of all the forces that make for a better world, none is so indispensable, none so powerful as hope.

Without hope men are only half-alive. With hope they dream, think and work.

~ Charles Sawyer ~

Mind must be rich

The human mind cannot create anything. It produces nothing until after having been fertilised by experience and meditation; its acquisitions are the gems of its production.

~ Buffon ~

Human beings cause sorrows for themselves

Most of the sorrows of the earth
humans cause for themselves.

~ Jack Kornfield ~

Mind creates evil
Evil springs from the mind;
Then it turns on the mind and robs it.
Evil is like rust on iron;
Slowly it destroys the form.

~ Fo Shuo Pei Sutra ~

Mind over body
The mind controls the body.
The body does not control the mind.
The mind can fool the body and
it can kill the body.

~ Buddha - Dig ~

Good weapons
You need two good weapons;
A heart that is pure,
A will that is ready,
To do and endure!

Nature of the Mind

If mind is correct, everything is correct

If your mind is in balance,
What need is there to work at morality?
If your mind is pure,
What use is meditation to you?

~ Sixth Patriarch ~

Likes and dislikes

People are slaves to their likes and dislikes,
So much so that they cannot see straight.
Likes and dislikes are
two extremes created by the mind.
In between is the neutral gear.

~ Lessons in Enlightenment ~

Disappointment

With expectation comes disappointment.

The difficulty to know the truth

Truth is simple — Mind is complex.

The sleep of delusion

People dream day and night.
They get carried away by their dreams.
Life becomes complicated and difficult.
The practice of mindfulness/
awareness lights up their being.
Their being sees through their dreams.
Waking up from the sleep of delusion,
They realise the nature of mundane existence.
Now they are ready to step out of the mind,
and go beyond.
Liberation at last from the ills of life.

~ Lesson in Enlightenment ~

Changing minds

- A mind that is fast is sick.
- A mind that is slow is sound.
- A mind that is still is divine.

~ Meher Baba ~

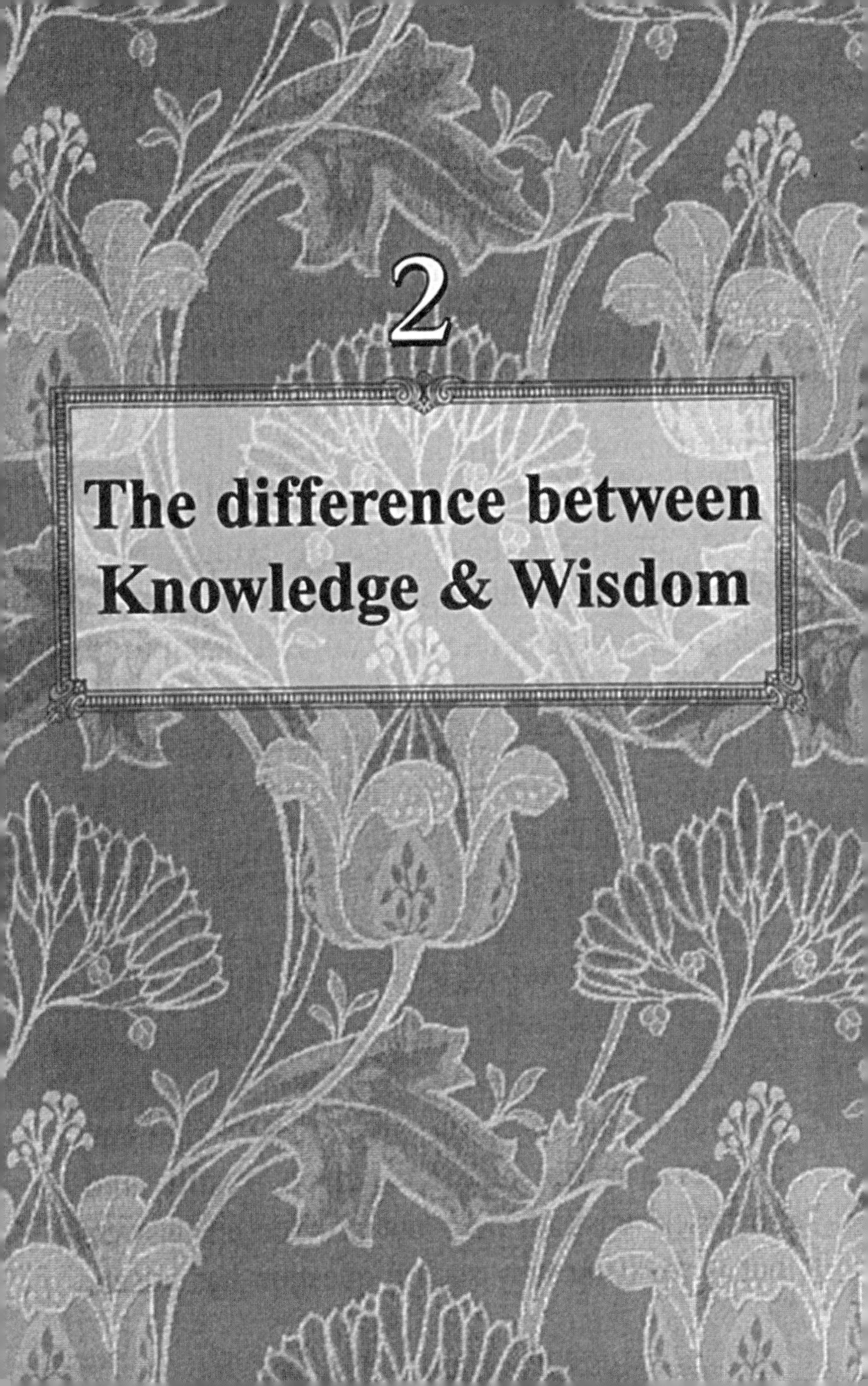

2

The difference between Knowledge & Wisdom

FOOD FOR THE THINKING MIND

Knowledge is something which has been defined as 'justified true belief', and which is studied in the branch of philosophy known as epistemology. The quest for knowledge knows no boundaries. There is no limit to pursuing knowledge, because knowledge is clearly different from 'feeling sure' about what exists or about the course of events. Most philosophical debate on the subject centres on the nature of truth and on what counts as appropriate evidence for claiming to know something. In Buddhist teaching, there are three sources of knowledge: Inference, Perception and Experience.

Knowledge of how things work is quite different from realisation which is wisdom, which is insight, which wants to see why it works, and how it works. Wisdom is so much more than knowledge. Knowledge is the answer to the question how? Wisdom is investigation of the answer to the question why? Knowledge can answer a query about function, result, and purposes: wisdom does not provide an answer, but is realising why such a question has arisen.

And in that realisation of the question, there is no search beyond because insight has solved the problem, dissolved the conflict and ended the search. Thus, where knowledge searches outside, wisdom ceases at the insight into the question.

The Buddha was once asked as to whether without sensuous pleasure life would be endurable; without belief in immortality man could be moral and without worship of a God man could advance towards righteousness. The Buddha replied in the affirmative and mentioned that these ends could be attained by knowledge; knowledge alone was the key to the higher path, the one worth pursuing in life; knowledge was that which brought calmness and peace to life, which rendered man indifferent to the storms of the phenomenal world.

Education

Every person has two education, one which he received from others, and one, more important, which he gives himself.

~ Gibbon ~

Visions and ideals

He who cherished a beautiful vision, lofty ideals in his heart, will one day realise it. Columbus cherished a vision of another world, and he discovered it; Copernicus fostered the vision of a multiplicity of worlds and a wider universe, and he revealed it; Buddha beheld the vision of a spiritual world of stainless beauty and perfect peace, and he entered into it.

~ Dale Carnegie ~

Education corrects

Education polishes good dispositions and corrects bad ones.

Solitude and wisdom

Solitude is the nurse of wisdom.

Wisdom lingers

Knowledge comes, but wisdom lingers.

~ Lord Tennyson ~

What is real education?

The word educate has its roots in the Latin word 'educo' which means to educe, to draw out, to develop from within.

The best-educated man is the one whose mind has been the most highly developed.

~ Napoleon Hill ~

Why man needs education

Man is essentially selfish and evil and therefore needs education and culture in order to be good.

Even then, however, he does not derive the principles of virtue from a divine being but from that, which is a special phenomenon.

~ Hsun Tzu ~

Man must learn

Man is not a being born only to live in society. As Aristotle said, "He is also a being born to acquire, communicate and accumulate knowledge."

Collect little by little

Even a pot is filled gradually by little drops of water. So should one acquire knowledge and wealth.

~ Hitopadesa ~

Knowledge dispels fear and worry

Fear and worry disappear when ignorance is dispelled by knowledge.

Human reason and cosmic reason

Just as our bodies are composed of some matter to be found throughout the universe, so must our human reason be part of a universal cosmic reason.

~ Socrates ~

Who is the real fool?

The fool who does not admit he is a fool, is a real fool.

And the fool who admits he is a fool is wise to that extent at least.

~ Buddha - Dh. ~

A man who has only one eye for him to see

A man, blind in one eye went to a cinema to buy a ticket to see a movie. He asked for a half-rate ticket.

The manager asked, "Why half-rate?" He replied, "All the others use two eyes to see the movie but I use only one eye!"

Proper understanding towards wrongdoers

If a man does something wrong to you through his ignorance or misunderstanding, that is the most opportune time for you to use your wisdom, your education, and understanding.

Kind-hearted fools

Kindness, honesty and patience without common sense are fertile grounds for cunning people to take advantage of those who possess such good qualities. Some people regard them as kind-hearted fools.

Evil doers are ignorant

Many people perform evil because of ignorance rather than wickedness by nature. As such, they need guidance rather than punishment.

Second class human beings

People who do not think for themselves and always borrow ideas from others are second-class human beings.

~ Krishnamurti ~

Belief and thinking

Those who believe do not think.

Those who think do not believe.

~ Sigmund Freud ~

Those who never change their minds

Very intelligent men and really stupid men both do not change their minds.

~ Confucius ~

You can learn from your enemies too

You should not think that you could only learn from those who praise you, help you, and associate with you very closely. You also could learn many things from your enemies. You should not think they are entirely wrong just because they happened to be your enemies. They may also possess certain good qualities.

Knowledge is not free from ignorance

All our superficial knowledge based on our senses is really ignorance, and true knowledge is only obtained by shedding all this until we think without using sense ideas.

~ A French Scholar ~

Enemies reveal your mistakes

Do not hate your enemies for they will reveal your faults.

Realisation comes not only through experience but by thinking

A shoal of fish came across an obstruction with an unusually small opening in the water. It was a trap laid by a fisherman to catch fish. Some fishes wanted to go inside to see what it was, but the more experienced fishes advised them not to do so because it could be a dangerous trap.

A young fish asked, "How do we know whether it is dangerous or not? We must go in and see. Only then can we understand what it is." So some of them went in and got caught in the trap.

Prejudice arises from ignorance

Prejudice is the child of ignorance.

Through new problems one can forget old problems

We usually create some other problems while trying to solve our existing ones. If the new problem is minor, we tolerate it to the best of our ability and do what we can to alleviate the pain. Sometimes a 'give and take policy' also helps to settle our problems. It is impossible to settle all our problems because problems are like waves. When one wave calms down, it will create the force for another to go up.

How grave is our folly

To the fire flies, the moth
Knowing not it will die.
Little fish bites the hook,
Knowing not of the danger.
But though knowing well the danger

Of these evil worldly pleasures,
We still cling to them so firmly.
Oh how great is our folly!

Today the light of knowledge is shining

The humans of the modern era are fortunate in being born at a time when the light of knowledge is shining with considerable lustre.

It is, therefore, an insult to our human dignity that we are utilising that light not to improve our mind but to destroy ourselves along with our environment.

It is also of paramount importance that all the media available in modern times, be mobilised to save lives and civilisation.

Two kinds of fools

Those who abuse their intellect are called intellectual fools and those who develop emotional kindness without reasoning are called kind-hearted fools.

Buddha also says that there are two kinds of fools: those who undertake unnecessary burdens and those who do not undertake necessary responsibilities.

Learning and thought must work together

Learning without thought is naught;
thought without learning is dangerous.

~ Confucius ~

Knowledge and morality

In Buddhism, there can be no real morality without knowledge, no real knowledge without morality; both are bound up together like heat and light in a flame.

What constitutes 'Bodhi' is enlightenment with compassion. The consciousness of moral excellence is the very essence of 'Bodhi'.

Fear dominates a fool's mind

Wheresoever fear arises,
it arises in the fool,
not in the wise man.
Wisdom comes through
the recognition of ignorance.

~ Buddha ~

Rare is the noble wise man

Hard to find is a man of great wisdom:
such a man is not born everywhere.
Where such a wise man is born,
that family thrives happily.

~ Buddha ~

How I understood myself

At forty, I had no more doubts.
At fifty, I knew the will of heaven.
At sixty, I was ready to listen to it.
At seventy, I could follow my heart's desire
Without transgressing what was right.

~ Confucius ~

Try to understand yourself

To understand yourself
is the beginning of wisdom.
You must try to know
who you are without depending on others.

Education is learning to be disciplined

Education does not mean teaching people to know what they do not know; it means teaching them to behave as they do not behave.

~ John Ruskin ~

Experience comes through mistakes

Experience is the name everyone
gives to their mistakes.

~ Oscar Wilde ~

A wise man is quiet

The quiet man is not necessarily wise,
but usually the wise man is quiet.

Knowledge comes from many sources

A student acquires a quarter of his knowledge from his teacher, another quarter from his own intelligence, the third quarter from his co-students and the last quarter in course of time from experience.

~ *Mahabharata* ~

Learning has its own rewards

From learning comes humility,
Humility makes one receptive,
To be receptive is to prosper,
Prosperity leads to dharma and joy.

~ *Hitopadesa* ~

Philosophy and Buddhism

Philosophy deals mainly with knowledge and is not concerned with practice, whereas Buddhism lays special emphasis on practice and realisation based on understanding.

Therefore, the concern of philosophy is to know and that of Buddhism is to practise.

When you understand yourself, you understand everything

When you try to understand everything,
You will not understand anything.
When you understand yourself,
You will understand everything.

~ Shunryn Suzuki ~

Thinking man

Thinking man has been a long time
on the road of evolution,
and he has travelled a very long way.

~ Napoleon Hill ~

Inspiration is an important part of learning

A teacher who is attempting to teach without inspiring the pupil with a desire to learn is hammering on cold iron.

~ Horace Mann ~

What man thinks, he becomes

A man is but the product of his thoughts; what he thinks, he becomes.

~ Mahatma Gandhi ~

The remedy for weakness

Instead of worrying about your problems, try to find out where the mistake is. The remedy for weakness is not brooding over weakness, but thinking of strength.

~ Swami Vivekananda ~

Knowledge is not wisdom

Wisdom is not knowledge. We do gain knowledge after listening, reading, and observing many things in this world but it is not wisdom in the real sense. Wisdom only appears in the mind when mental hindrances, obstructions and other impurities are not active in the mind.

There are many learned people all over the world that, no doubt, have wonderful knowledge, but unfortunately, some lack proper wisdom. They are intelligent but their behaviour is questionable. They may be hot-tempered, egoistic, emotional, jealous, greedy and temperamental.

On the other hand, there are others who are very kind, patient, tolerant and have many other good qualities. However, they lack wisdom and can be easily misled by others. If we develop generosity without proper knowledge, we could get into trouble when people take advantage of us. Knowledge and good qualities must, therefore, go together.

Knowledge is of three kinds

- that acquired by learning,
- that acquired by thinking, and
- that acquired by meditation.

This is wisdom, which is the apex of the threefold training — discipline, concentration, and wisdom — leading to ultimate bliss.

Do not rely on miracles

Do not rely upon the performance of miracles for the attainment of the object of your definite chief aim; rely upon the power of infinite intelligence to guide you, through natural channels, and with the aid of natural laws, for its attainment.

Do not expect infinite intelligence to bring to you the object of your definite chief aim; instead, expect infinite intelligence to direct you toward that object.

~ Napoleon Hill ~

Do not cling to your beliefs

O Bhikkus, even this view
(Teaching of the Buddha)
Which is so pure and so clear,
If you cling to it,
If you fondle it,
If you treasure it,
If you are attached to it,
Then you do not understand

That the teaching is similar to a raft,
Which is for crossing over and
Not for getting hold of.

~ Buddha - M. I: 260; Miln: 316 ~

Nature of a wise man

He who has understanding and great wisdom does not think of harming himself or another, nor harming both alike. He rather thinks of his own welfare, that of others, that of both, and that of the welfare of the whole world.

~ Buddha - A. IV ~

Difficulty of understanding the real truth

A great truth, sometimes, appears so simple that it fails to make an impression and therefore, takes a long time to be realised.

~ Spanish proverb ~

Age and wisdom

Wisdom does not necessarily come with age.

Be patient

Patience is the companion of wisdom.

~ St. Augustine ~

How to gain strength

Strength is born in the deep silence
of long suffering hearts; not amid joy.

~ Mrs Herman ~

What is soft is strong

Water is fluid, soft and yielding. But water will wear away rock, which is rigid and cannot yield.

As a rule, whatever is fluid, soft and yielding will overcome whatever is rigid and hard. This is another paradox: what is soft is strong.

~ Lao Tze ~

Softness can overcome hardness

The softest thing in the world can overcome the hardest thing in the world.

Beginning of wisdom

Kindness is more important than wisdom,
and the recognition of this is
the beginning of wisdom.

~ Theodore Isaac Rubin ~

Real contentment

When the sun rises, I work.
When the sun sets, I rest.
I dig my well for water;
I till the land for food;
What care I the power of the Emperor.

~ Chinese saying ~

The foundation of knowledge

The fountain of knowledge does not spring accidentally. Educators who seek ways to quench mankind's thirst for knowledge dig it through layers of ignorance.

Knowledge — what we know — means little unless intelligently applied to serve others!

What lies within us?

What lies behind us and what lies before us are tiny matters compared to what lies within us.

~ Oliver Wendell Hodges ~

Learning and thought

Learning without thought is labour lost;
thought without learning is perilous.

~ Confucius ~

The means of education

The things taught in schools and colleges are not an education, but the means of education.

~ R. W. Emerson ~

How does man become wise?

The Yaksha asked, "By the study of which science does man become wise?"

Yudhishthra replied, "Not by studying any book does man become wise. It is by association with the great in wisdom that he gets wisdom."

~ *Mahabharata* ~

We give a lot of advice but we take little

We give advice to others by the bucket,
but take it by the grain.

~ *W. R. Alger* ~

He who fails to know himself misses everything

He who would know everything, but fails to know himself misses the knowledge of everything.

~ *Jesus Christ* ~

The thoughtful man wins her

A handsome man attracts a woman.
An intelligent man interests her.
A humorous man amuses her.
An attentive man flatters her.
A generous man pleases her.

An honest man surprises her.
The thoughtful man wins her.

Little knowledge

If little knowledge is dangerous, where is the man who has so much as to be out of danger?

~ Thomas Huxley ~

Study and observe

To acquire knowledge one must study, but to acquire wisdom one must observe.

~ Marilyn Savant ~

Learning can increase ignorance

The more we learn about things existing in the world, the more we create our own concepts and fantasies, which are the products of our limited way of thinking and shaped by our limited senses. Instead of gaining wisdom, we increase our ignorance.

The difference between Knowledge & Wisdom

People who claim to know many things only develop their egoism and sceptical views, which create more confusion and disturb the peace and confidence in their minds.

The knowledge and attitude they maintain often create more misunderstanding and conflict instead of generating harmony and goodwill.

~ A French Scholar ~

Good manners open doors

Good manners will open doors
that the best education cannot.

~ Clarence Thomas ~

Good short life is more valuable

Better to live a single day with wisdom, bright, contemplative than live for a hundred years unwise and unconcentrated.

~ Buddha - Dh. ~

Ambitions never reach the top

As dogs in a wheel, or squirrels in a cage, ambitious men still climb and climb with greater labour and incessant anxiety, but never reach the top.

~ Burton ~

Education is sweet

The roots of education are bitter,
but the fruit is sweet.

~ Aristotle ~

Mirror reflects all objects

The mirror reflects all objects,
without being sullied.

~ Confucius ~

Nothing can be done

A conference is a gathering of important people who singly can do nothing, but together can decide that nothing can be done.

Honesty creates real friends

You cannot believe in other people unless you yourself are honest. If you tell lies and are always trying to outwit others, you inevitably will assume that everyone else also is a liar and trickster. You never will be able to enjoy true friendship.

~ Vision ~

Mind your own business

Once, some woodcutters were cutting a fallen tree trunk. They began by splitting the trunk down the middle. To make their work easier, they inserted a wedge between the two parts as they proceeded. As it was almost noon, they decided to take a break, leaving the tree trunk with the wedge still in place. Just then a monkey came along. He wanted to know what the wedge was doing there, so he sat astride the trunk, with his tail (and other organs!) hanging between the spilt trunk. After shaking the wedge vigorously, he succeeded in removing it, but in so doing, the two sides of the trunk slammed shut crushing his tail and his other organs and killing him.

Foolish corner in the mind

There is a foolish corner even in the brain of a sage.

~ Aristotle ~

Failure is our teacher

Failure is not fatal. Failure should be our teacher, not our undertaker. It should challenge us to new heights of accomplishments, not pull us to new depths of despair. From honest failure can come valuable experience.

~ Wilfred H. Peterson ~

Knowledge without serving others is not useful

Knowledge — what we know — means little unless intelligently applied to serve others!

Learn life's hard lesson

From life's experience we must learn.
For life's hard lessons unlearned leave us fossilised and impotent in a desert of ignorance.

Fear appears due to lack of understanding

Every kind of fear grows worse by not being looked at. The effort of turning away one's thoughts (like the ostrich with its head in the sand), is a tribute to the horribleness of the spectre from which one is averting one's gaze; the proper course with every kind of fear is to think about it rationally and calmly, but with great concentration, until it becomes completely familiar.

In the end, familiarity will blunt its terrors; the whole subject will become boring, and our thoughts will turn away from it, not as formerly by an effort of will, but through mere lack of interest in the topic. When you find yourself inclined to brood on anything, no matter what, the best plan always is to think about it even more than you naturally would, until at last its morbid fascination is worn off.

~ Bertrand Russell ~

Middle Way

Everything in moderation,
including moderation.

~ Jack Kornfield ~

Who knows?

No one knows everything.
No one knows nothing.
Everyone knows something.

How to think

Thinking is the hardest work there is,
which is the probable reason
why so few engage in it.

~ Henry Ford ~

Common sense

Common sense in an uncommon degree
is what the world calls wisdom.

~ Samuel Coleridge ~

How to reach the moon without spending anything

When the Americans landed on the moon, Mao Zedong in China said, "We can reach the moon without spending anything. When people asked, "How?" He said, "We have enough people in our country to climb onto each other to reach the moon!"

Answering the question by knowing the questioner's mind

A man, who had never seen a train, visited the railway station one day. Having seen the train engine running, he asked, "How can that one run without a horse? Where is the horse?" His friend knowing his mentality told him, "The horse runs inside the train." "No wonder, that is why I could not understand how the train runs."

Advantage of other's jealousy

When someone is jealous of you, he is paying you a compliment, though in an unpleasant way.

It is as if he is saying: "Look, you have something, which I do not have, I would like to have and I feel helpless at the thought that I cannot have it."

Blind cannot lead the blind

Can the blind lead the blind? Won't they both fall into a pit?

A student is not better than his teacher. It is enough for a student to be like his teacher.

~ Jesus Christ ~

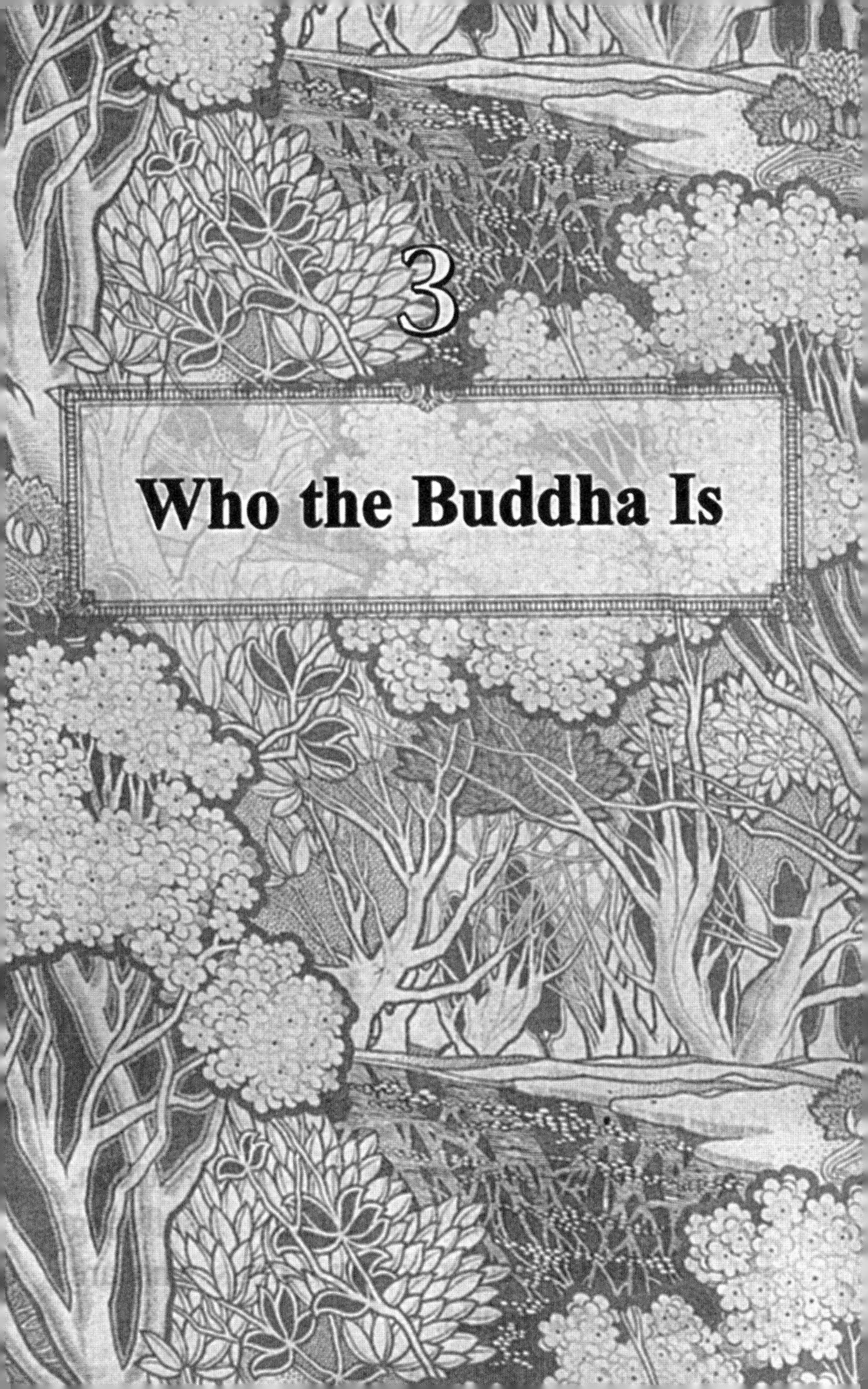

3

Who the Buddha Is

uddhahood is not reserved only for the chosen people or for the supernatural beings. Anyone can become a Buddha. No founder of any other religion ever said that his followers could have the opportunity or potentiality to attain the same position as the founder.

However, attaining Buddhahood is the most difficult task a person can pursue in this world. One must work hard by sacrificing one's worldly pleasures. One has to develop and purify one's mind from evil thoughts in order to obtain this enlightenment. It will take innumerable births for a person to purify himself and to develop his mind in order to become a Buddha. Long periods of great effort are necessary in order to complete the high qualification of this self-training. The course of this self-training which culminates in Buddhahood, includes self-discipline, self-restraint, superhuman effort, firm determination, and willingness to undergo any kind of suffering for the sake of other living beings who are suffering in this world.

This clearly shows that the Buddha did not obtain his supreme enlightenment by simply praying, worshipping, or making offerings to some supernatural beings. He attained Buddhahood by the purification of his mind and heart. He gained supreme enlightenment without the influence of any external supernatural forces but by the development of his own insight. Thus, only a man who has firm determination and courage to overcome all hindrances, weaknesses and selfish desires can attain Buddhahood.

The Buddha had a natural birth; he lived in a normal way. But he was an extraordinary man, as far as his enlightenment was concerned. Those who have not learnt to appreciate his supreme wisdom, try to explain his greatness by peeping into his life and looking for miracles. However, the Buddha's supreme enlightenment is more than enough for us to understand his greatness. There is no need to show his greatness by introducing any miraculous power. Every supernatural power becomes natural when people come to know how it takes place.

How to see the Buddha

One of the disciples of the Buddha named Vakkali had a habit of gazing upon him everyday.
The Buddha having noticed this asked, "What are you doing here?"
Vakkali's reply was "Venerable Sir, when I look at the serene features and good complexion of your body, that itself gives me a lot of satisfaction."
The Buddha then asked, "What do you expect to gain by admiring this body which is dirty, ugly, smelly, impermanent? One who sees the Dharma, sees the Buddha."

This should help you to understand how to see the real Buddha. If you indeed want to see the real Buddha, then you must reflect on that Buddha in your mind through the realisation of his teaching — the Dharma.

The life of the Buddha is a poem

The whole life story of the Buddha is a wonderful poem. It is so fascinating, attractive and artistic and I have never read such a wonderful poem. The emergence of the Buddha is the highest honour so far gained in the history of humanity.

~ *Rabindranath Tagore* ~

The Buddha had no teacher for gaining enlightenment

All have I overcome, I know.
From all am I detached! All have I renounced.
Wholly absorbed am I
in the destruction of craving.
Having comprehended all by myself.
Whom shall I call my teacher?

A teacher who never had human frailty

The Buddha was the embodiment of all the virtues he preached. His moral code is the most perfect the world has ever known. During his successful and eventful forty-five years as a supremely enlightened teacher, he translated all his work into essence and in no place did he give vent to any human frailty or any base passion.

~ Prof. Max Müller ~

In support of human dignity

The voice of the Buddha is the most powerful voice that has been heard in human history in support of the dignity of man and of the principle that man is the maker of his own destiny, and that man is not for religion but that religion must serve man.

That means: without becoming a slave to any religion, man must try to make use of religion for his betterment and liberation.

The voice that entertained everybody

Thanks to this voice, ordinary people are able to develop their faith and confidence, educated people have food for thought, and intellectuals have enriched their vision.

Those who were misguided had their views corrected. Those who have not relied on blind faith have received a clear vision of the Truth. Sceptics were persuaded and won over by the voice of reason. Devotees gained confidence, understanding and liberation from suffering.

Prince in beggar's clothing

If you desire to see the most noble of mankind, look at the prince in beggar's clothing; it is he whose sanctity is great among men – 'the Buddha'.

~ Abdul Atahiya ~

Everlasting value and advanced ethics

The Buddha gave expression to truths of everlasting value and advanced the ethics not of India alone but of humanity. The Buddha was one of the greatest ethical men of genius ever bestowed upon the world.

~ Albert Schweitzer ~

The god who walked on the earth

The Buddha is the only god who ever walked on this earth.

~ Swami Vivekananda ~

Buddha is not a myth

You see clearly a man, simple, devout, lonely, battling for light, a vivid human personality, and not a myth. He gave a message to mankind universal in its character. Many of our best modern ideas are in closest harmony with it.

~ H. G. Wells ~

Who are you?

One day, a Brahmin happened to meet the Buddha and he could not believe that he was a human being. He asked, "Are you a god?"
The Buddha said, "No."
He then asked, "Are you a supernatural being?"
The Buddha said, "No, I am very natural!"
In the end he asked, "Are you an ordinary human being?"

The Buddha said, "No."
The confused Brahmin asked, "Then who are you?"
The Buddha answered, "I am the Awakened One (Buddha)."

One who knows the true nature of the world

Among the founders of all religions in this world, I respect only one man — the Buddha. The main reason was that the Buddha did not make statements regarding the origin of the world. The Buddha was the only teacher who realised the true nature of the world.

But, while many others made unjustifiable claims based on rather simplistic logic on how the world originated, the Buddha did not commit himself to any statement about a beginning. This was because he knew his listeners did not have the proper intellectual training and understanding of the physical world to comprehend what he himself had discovered.

~ Bertrand Russell ~

The Buddha's self-introduction

Known are the things to be known,
Cultivated are the things to be cultivated,
Destroyed are the things to be destroyed,
Therefore, Brahmin, I am the Buddha.

One who has reached above all

Show me in history one character that has reached so high above all. The whole human race has produced but one such person - Buddha - preaching high philosophy yet having the deepest of sympathy even for the lowest animal.

~ Swami Vivekananda ~

The Buddha emphasised reason, morals, principles and experience

The Buddha had the courage to point out the unsatisfactoriness of popular religion, superstition, ceremony, and priest craft. He was not interested in the metaphysical and theological outlook, miracles, revelations, and dealings with the supernatural. His appeal was to reason, logic, and experience; his emphasis was on ethics and his method was one of psychological analysis, a psychology without a soul. His whole approach comes like the breath of the fresh wind from the mountain after the stale air of metaphysical speculation.

~ Pandit Nehru ~

The noble example of the Buddha

The Buddha's noble example was a source of inspiration to all his iron will, profound wisdom, universal love, boundless compassion, selfless service, historic renunciation, perfect purity, and magnetic personality have inspired people to respect him as a world-honoured Supreme Teacher!

Flower of mankind

This is the Blossom on our human tree
Which opens once in many myriad years —
But when opened, fills the world with

Wisdom's scent and Love's dropped honey.

~ Sir Edwin Arnold ~

Eternal debt to the Buddha

It is my deliberate opinion that the essential part of the teachings of the Buddha now forms an integral part of Hinduism. It is impossible for Hindu India today to retrace her steps and go behind the great reformation that Gautama effected in Hinduism.

By his immense sacrifice, by his great renunciation, and by the immaculate purity of his life he left an indelible impression upon Hinduism, and Hinduism owes an eternal debt of gratitude to that great teacher.

~ Mahatma Gandhi ~

Who are close to the Buddha?

There may be many disciples who stay with me, follow me by holding my hand or clinging to my robes, thereby, thinking that they are close to me. On the other hand, there may be some other disciples who are far away from me and who have not even seen me, but if their minds are pure, even though they are staying far away, they are indeed very close to me. Those who stay with me but exist only with polluted minds, are in fact not at all close to me.

~ Buddha ~

The Buddha's way of seeing human suffering

The Buddha's approach to the problems of human suffering is essentially empirical and experimental and not speculative and metaphysical.

The greatest conqueror of the world

The Buddha was the greatest conqueror the world has ever seen. He conquered the world with his infallible weapons of compassion and wisdom. His teaching illuminates the way for mankind to cross from a world of darkness, hatred and suffering, to a New World of light, love, happiness and security.

~ Dr. Malalasekara ~

Buddha's message to humanity

The Buddha has been something greater than all doctrines and dogmas, and his eternal message has thrilled humanity through the ages. Perhaps at no time in past history was his message of peace more needed for a suffering and distracted humanity than it is today.

~ Pandit Nehru ~

The Buddha's voice comforted suffering poor

The voice of the Buddha has comforted the bereaved and helped the suffering poor. It has ennobled the lives of the deluded and purified the corrupted lives of criminals. It has encouraged the feeble, united the divided, enlightened the ignorant, elevated the base and dignified the noble.

~ *Prof. Max Müller* ~

The voice of the Buddha is not a voice from heaven

He belongs to the history of the world's thought, to the general inheritance of all cultivated men; for, judged by intellectual integrity, moral earnestness, and spiritual insight, he is undoubtedly the greatest human being who has ever lived.

This was not the heavenly voice of a divine power, but a very human voice, which called on men to seek final emancipation through mental purification and enlightenment. Even today, this voice echoes in our ears and reminds us that we can understand the truth revealed by him, if only we exercise our will and our concentration.

The voice of the Buddha is a message of hope, confidence and courage. It tells us that hatred never ceases through hatred but only by loving-kindness. This vibrant voice emanated from a great personality, who was once a warrior, a royal prince, a yogi, a mendicant and finally a Buddha.

~ *Prof. Max Müller* ~

Buddha as a saviour

The Buddha is not a saviour in the same sense that others believe in a saviour, yet Buddhists regard him a saviour since he has shown the path for humanity to save themselves.

The Buddha for everybody

To great philosophers and unbiased thinkers, he is a teacher who understood worldly conditions in their proper perspective.

To moralists, he has the highest code of discipline and he symbolises perfection.

To rationalists, he is the most liberal minded religious teacher who understood vexing human problems.

To free thinkers, he is a religious teacher who

encouraged people to think freely without depending on religious dogmas.

- To agnostics, he is a very intelligent, kind, understanding and peace-loving man.
- To Hindus, he is an incarnation of their god.
- To socialists, he is a social reformer.
- To religious devotees, he is a holy man.

Buddhism begins where science ends

The Buddha is the pillar of wisdom and Buddhism begins where science ends. Buddhism is the complete conceivable victory of mankind over itself.

The Buddhists' way of thinking belongs to the future.

~ *Julius Huxley* ~

He raised the nobility of mankind

As a man, he attained Buddhahood and pro-claimed to the world the latent possibilities and the creative power of man. Instead of placing an unseen supernatural being over man and making him subservient to him, he raised the worth of mankind.

The Buddha's attitude towards gods

When a disciple of the Buddha asked whether there is any evidence to prove the existence of gods, the Buddha asked whether there is any evidence to disprove the existence of gods.

The calm Buddha image

His eyes are closed but some power of the spirit looks out of them and a vital energy fills the frame.

The ages roll by and Buddha seems not so far away after all; his voice whispers in our ears and tells us not to run away from the struggle but calmed-eyed, to face it, and to see in life even greater opportunities for growth and advancement.

~ Pandit Nehru ~

The humble attitude of the Buddha

Kings, ministers and multi-millionaires approached the Buddha to pay their homage and seek guidance. But he, himself, visited and used his persuasive voice to enlighten sweepers, cobblers, thieves, gangsters, murderers, courtesans and many others who were leading hard, wicked and immoral lives to mend their ways and lead noble lives.

The Buddha's attitude towards evil doers

The more evil that comes to me,
the more good will radiate from me.

What the Buddha image teaches us

It seems that the kindly, appreciative, eternally young man is seated cross-legged on the lotus of purity with his right hand raised in admonition to utter these words: "If you wish to escape from suffering, from fear, practise compassion and develop wisdom."

~ *Anatole France* ~

Why the Buddha kept silence

When metaphysical questions were asked, he often did not reply, not because the Buddha had nothing to say but because he had far too much to say, which would only confuse the questioner.

The riddle-mongers of his day posed questions which were both too narrow and too shallow to answer for gaining wisdom or spiritual development.

The Buddha taught self-reliance

Of all the teachers of the world, the Buddha was the one who taught us to be self-reliant, who freed us not only from the bondage of our views but from the dependence on invisible beings called god or gods.

He invited everyone into the state of freedom, which he called Nirvana. All must attain it one day and the attainment is the complete fulfilment of man.

~ Swami Vivekananda ~

Why Buddha is needed for our salvation

It was the Buddha who taught that man could gain his own salvation by his own exertion without depending on God or mediating priest.

Buddhists do not take refuge in the Buddha seeking salvation directly through him, but to gain guidance and confidence for salvation.

The Buddha's early morning duty

May my heart lend its ear to every cry of pain,
As the lotus bares its heart
to drink the morning sun.
Let not the fierce sun dry one tear of pain,
Before I wipe it off from the sufferer's eyes.
But let each burning human tear
Drop on my heart and there remain,
Nor ever be brushed off until the pain
That caused it is removed.

~ *Rabindranath Tagore* ~

How to gain salvation?

Do not depend on others for your salvation
Develop your self-confidence to gain it.

~ Buddha - M ~

Devotees gain the same good results whether Buddha exists or not

Whether the Buddha lives or has attained Nibbana,
The fruit is the same if
The mind of the giver is the same.
For having delight in the Buddha
Beings go to heavenly birth.

~ Expositor ~

Salvation never comes from another person

It is not the Buddha who delivers living beings. He guides them to deliver themselves, even as he has delivered himself. They accept his teaching of the truth, not because it comes from him, but because personal conviction, inspired by his words, arises by the light of their own spirit.

~ Dr. Oldenburg ~

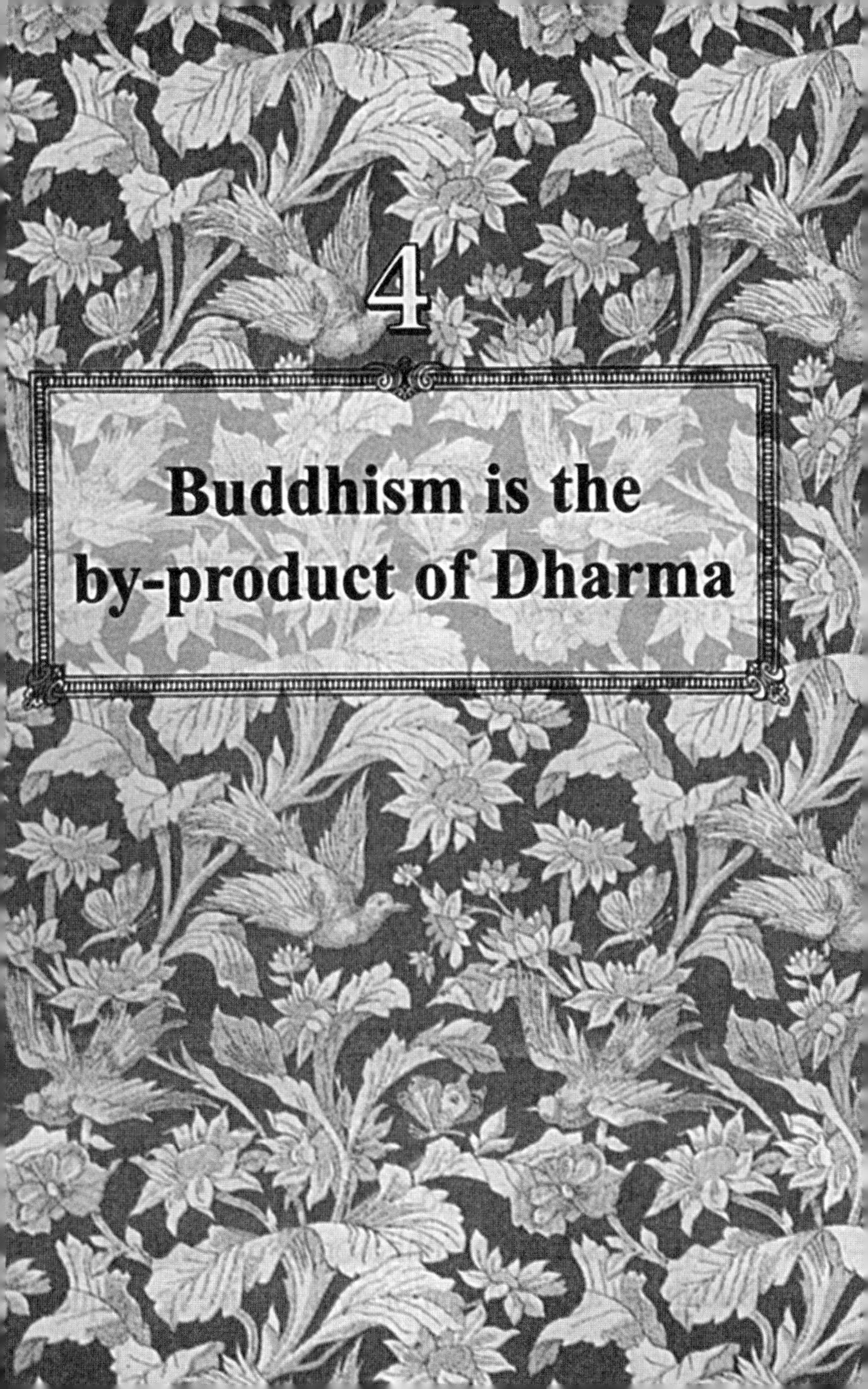

4

Buddhism is the by-product of Dharma

harma means truth, that which really is; it also means law — the law which exists in a man's own heart and mind; it is the principle of righteousness; therefore, the Buddha advises to man to be noble, pure and worthy of honour. Dharma, this law of righteousness, exists not only in a man's heart and mind, but it exists in the universe also. The etymological meaning of the word is 'that which upholds or supports', therefore Dharma is every principle on which the cosmos operates.

The entire universe is an embodiment or revelation of the Dharma. The law of nature which modern science has discovered is the revelations of Dharma, for Dharma is that law within the universe which makes matter act in the way studied in physics, chemistry, zoology, botany and astronomy. Dharma exists in the universe just as gravity, wind and heat. The teaching of the Buddha is called Dharma because he explained how natural occurrences take place according to worldly conditions and universal law.

Buddhism is the philosophy of awakening. Buddhism as a religion or as a science is unique in the importance it attaches to philosophy and metaphysical inquiry. As such, it is often regarded as the most advanced of the philosophic systems of India. Ethics, science and philosophy are delicately interwoven into a system, which is divorced from mythology and which attempts to unravel the real nature of life.

There is no aspect of the Buddha-Dharma, or the Buddhist teachings, which does not stem from the logical and rational foundations of that philosophy. The Buddha Dharma is to pave the way for final salvation by leading a noble life.

Buddhism may be defined as a way of life, called the Noble Eightfold Path, leading to a goal called Nirvana. This goal or deliverance is the state of supreme good, because it is free from defects, and has ultimate peace, purity, and the highest happiness that our minds can conceive. Yet, it is something, which cannot be conferred by another person, however exalted he or she may be, but must be won by one's own effort. Buddhism teaches the principle that everything in the world comes on account of something else. There is no first event or first cause.

Many meanings of the word "Dharma"

- Nature
- Teaching
- Doctrine
- Wisdom
- Intelligence
- Justice
- Right way
- Truth
- Norm
- Usual
- Primary condition or state
- Merit, meritorious deeds
- Virtue, good conduct or good manners, civility
- Concentration, mental disciplines
- Non-being, non-self
- Transgression
- Disciplinary code
- Law

Dharma is above all

No one is above the Dharma. Even the Buddha himself cannot change the Dharma. Dharma is the unconditioned universal law.

Dharma is like a wondrous herb that heals the sick

The Buddha opens the gate to liberation to all without discrimination. Caste, class, race, sex or religious labels meant little to him. All can benefit from the Dharma if we strive diligently to cultivate virtue, self-discipline and the mind. The Dharma is like a wondrous herb that heals the sick, regardless of their labels or social, cultural or political affiliations.

~ Prof. Max Müller ~

Life and universal laws

According to the Buddha, what human beings need for happiness and liberation are not mere religious beliefs, rituals or mass theories, but the knowledge of the Dharma: universal nature or cosmic nature and complete harmony with the law of cause and effect. Until this principle is fully understood, life is only an imperfect and unpredictable manifestation of its own nature.

The essence of the Dharma

In its most basic formulation, the essence of the Dharma, the Buddha's teaching, is *sila, samadhi* and *panna* — moral discipline, mental development and enlightenment.

Dharma is not appreciated by everybody

- This Dharma is for one who wants little,
  not for one who wants much.
- This Dharma is for the contented,
  not for the discontented.
- This Dharma is for the secluded,
  not for one who wastes time in the society.
- This Dharma is for the energetic,
  not for the lazy.
- This Dharma is for the mindful,
  and not for the unmindful.
- This Dharma is for the composed,
  not for the flustered.
- This Dharma is for the wise,
  not for the unwise.

~ Buddha ~

Three characteristics in everything

The three characteristics of everything in this universe are clearly explained only in Buddhism.

They are the impermanency of everything, the unsatisfactoriness of everything, and the impersonality or insubstantiality of everything. This is the most remarkable discovery of the Buddha. But due to ignorance and craving, there are very few people who can comprehend such a lofty and sublime teaching.

The wheel of existence and suffering

It is evident that the world is full of various kinds of sufferings, such as decay, sorrow, lamentation, pain, despair and death. The Buddha pointed out that birth (*jati*) brings forth sufferings. If there is no birth, there is no scope for suffering.

Q: Why is there birth?

A: The sub-conscious process of becoming (*bhava*) as a combination of mind and body (*nama-rupa*) causes birth. In other words, where there is bhava, there is birth.

Q: What leads to the formation of the

combination mind and body?

A: Clinging (*upadana*) leads to the mind-body combination.

Q: What leads to clinging?

A: Craving (*tanha*) leads to clinging.

Q: What produces craving?

A: Craving is produced by sensations or feeling (*vedana*).

Q: What generates feeling?

A: It is the contact (*phassa*) — of the senses with their objects — which generates feeling.

Q: What causes contact?

A: The six sense-bases (*salayatana*) are the causes of contact.

Q: How do the six sense-bases come into being?

A: Psycho-physical combination (*nama-rupa*) brings forth the six sense-bases.

Q: How does psycho-physical combination come into being?

A: With the appearance of inactive or passive consciousness (*vinnana* or *vipaka citta*) the psycho-physical combination comes into being.

Q: How does passive consciousness appear?

A: It is the outcome of latent Karmic energies (*sankhara*).

~ Paticca Samuppada ~

Beginning of the world

There is no reason to suppose that the world had a beginning at all. The idea that things must have a beginning is really due to the poverty of our imagination.

Therefore, perhaps, I need not waste any more time upon the argument about the first cause.

~ Bertrand Russell ~

Wisdom and virtue are inseparable twins

Wisdom is purified by virtue,
and virtue is purified by wisdom.
The virtuous person has wisdom,
and the wise person has virtue.
The combination of virtue and
wisdom is called the highest thing in the world.

~ Buddha - D. I: 84 ~

Buddhist philosophy

As much as man's understanding capacity is deep, Buddhist philosophy is the only teaching that can penetrate into the bottom of that deep knowledge.

~ Dr. Radhakrishnan ~

You too can attain the final goal

It is through unshaken perseverance
That I have reached the final goal
and enlightenment.
Through unceasing effort

that I have reached the peace supreme.
If you also will strive unceasingly,
You too will in time
attain the highest goal of bliss.

~ Buddha - M ~

Follow the Middle Path

Follow the middle path
In every aspect of your life,
Without extreme austerity or extreme indulgence
Especially when you practise a religion.

~ Buddha - S. V: 330 ~

Have contentment

They make no lamentation over the past,
They yearn not after that which is not come;
They satisfy themselves.
By depending on what they receive,
Hence comes it that they look serene of hue.

~ Buddha - Sn: 71 ~

The Buddha's message

His message is basically simple and meaningful: To put an end to evil; to do good in order to reduce defilements from the mind; and to develop the mind for complete purification.

No secret teaching in Buddhism

O Bhikkhus, the Dharma and the precepts taught by the Buddha send forth a clear light. Never are they observed in secrecy. They are as clear and evident 'as the sun-disk or the moon-disk'.

Furthermore, regarding the Dharma taught by the Buddha, 'there exists no closed fist of the teacher'. This means that the Buddha as a teacher kept no secrets in his teaching. Accordingly, there are no secrets or mysteries in Buddhism, which must be accepted unquestioningly by a follower on the basis of blind faith.

Buddhism stands majestically

In spite of the ravages of time and destruction

by Indian and foreign fanatics, Buddhism is still speaking vividly and majestically.

Through its thousands of inscriptions, about one thousand rock-cut sanctuaries and monasteries, thousands of ruined stupas and monastic establishments, and an incalculable number of images, sculptures, paintings and emblems, teachings prevailed universally among the classes and masses of India for over fifteen centuries after the age of the Buddha.

~ Dr. L. M. Joshi ~

Buddhism rejected many religious beliefs that India had

Buddhism is a rebel child of Hinduism.

~ Swami Vivekananda ~

Buddhism can exist even without any material object

The damages to Buddhist objects and places have been done. However, as long as people follow the Buddha's advice, his teaching or Dharma will continue to exist in the minds of the people. The Buddha's teachings can survive even if the images, pagodas, monasteries and books are destroyed.

The material side of Buddhism can always be reconstructed for so long as the teachings are still within the minds of the people.

Buddhism and religion

Buddhism is not strictly a religion in the sense in which that word is commonly understood, for it is not 'a system of faith and worship' and does not owe any allegiance to a supernatural being.

But it is a noble way of life for human beings to maintain human dignity and give credit to human intelligence.

Buddhism and world civilisation

Western historians such as H. G. Wells have admitted that Buddhism has done more for the advancement of world civilisation and true culture than any other influence in the chronicles of mankind, and that much that is best in other religions, has been drawn from Buddhism, while none of them has matched it in purity of ideas and nobility of teaching.

Buddhism and humanism

Buddhism is humanism where equality, morals, justice, freedom of thought, wisdom and peace reign supreme.

Humanism cannot be attained through the influence of external sources.

Buddhism and the parliamentary system

It may come as a surprise to many to learn that in the assemblies of the Buddhists two thousand five hundred years ago, are to be found the rudiments of our own parliamentary practice of the present day.

~ Lord Zeland, Viceroy of India ~

Buddhism and morality

Morality was considered necessary, since it alone could help in enforcing strict discipline and growth of one's personality. It stands at the apex of Buddha's religious and social philosophies.

Dr. B.R. Ambedkar says, "Morality is the essence of Dharma. Morality in Dharma arises from the direct necessity for man to love man. It does not require the sanction of God. It is not to please God that man has to be moral. It is for his own good and for the well-being of others that man has to love man."

How Buddhism was discovered

Buddhism is the direct result of a most intensive research, voluntarily conducted over a long period of time by a most kind-hearted, noble prince, who was imbued with infinite love and deep compassion for suffering beings.

It is not a message that is received from heaven. It should best be described as a mental therapy.

The aim of Buddhism

The aim of Buddhism is to release human beings from worldly suffering within the cycle of birth and death and guide them to achieve this liberation, without becoming slaves to certain beliefs and practices that people uphold in the name of religion.

A religion without persecution

There is no record known to me in the whole of the long history of Buddhism throughout the many centuries, where its followers have been for such lengthened periods been in supreme control, of any persecution by the Buddhists of the followers of any other faith.

~ Prof. Rhys Davids ~

Hinduism and Buddhism

Hindu systems of philosophy would have lost much of their depth, interest and value, if they had not assimilated much from Buddhism.

~ Dr. S. N. Dasgupta ~

What Hinduism had done to Buddhism

Hinduism threw away Buddhism after taking its essence.

~ Swami Vivekananda ~

Buddhism eliminates religious slavery

Buddhism can eliminate the darkness of ignorance and liberate the human being from the danger of his unconscious illusion and religious slavery. It can help man to become his own master.

Man can free himself from all evil if he can understand the nature of his own mind. In modern times, entertainments have been introduced to satisfy human emotions and relax the mind. They have become like drugs to create more excitement and restlessness in the mind arousing the hidden animal nature of the man.

The main purpose of religion is to calm the mind to reduce tension, excitement and fear from the mind.

Religious harmony in Buddhism

Another unique feature of Buddhism is its avoidance of quarrels with other religions or condemning other religions. Buddhism tries to reveal the truth. If aspects of this truth are found in other religions, Buddhism is ready to acknowledge it. This spirit of understanding is born not out of weakness but out of the strength of self-confidence.

The difficulties of crossing the ocean

One who has destroyed attachment
Along with hate and ignorance,
Has crossed the ocean — samsara
With its sharks and demons,
Its fearful waves so hard to cross.

~ Buddha - It. V ~

Buddhism and miracles

Changing the wicked or the cruel to be kind-hearted, a stingy person to be generous, a stupid person to be intelligent, a criminal to be saintly, a deceitful person to be honest and a lazy one to be energetic is the real miracle in the eyes of the Buddha. The performance of magic does not constitute miracles.

Reflect on yourself to know Buddhism

If you can understand the nature of your own mind, you can easily understand what Buddhism is. You may go round the world in search of Buddhism, but only when you concentrate and reflect on yourself, you will be able to find it. This is the method prescribed by the Buddha for self-realisation.

Man's wrong approach to security

In the wave of protest movements against everything, there is loss of moral standards, disintegration of family life, the intrusion of psychotic cults in art, music and fashion.

Today, man is seeking security, welfare and happiness in the wrong places, by wanting wrong things and by taking refuge in the wrong objects. In this present sad situation, Buddhism has much to offer.

Three aims of practising Buddhism

- To gain peace and happiness in this life,
- To have a contented and fortunate life hereafter,
- To achieve the ultimate aim of life: everlasting happiness and supreme bliss.

How to bring about real peace

Buddhism shows the path of peace, peace not of the grave but of the living, peace from out of deep understanding and proper appreciation of the realism of life.

Peace can only be permanent if it conquers evil and brings about a true harmony between spiritual and material impulses of man.

Sangha in Buddhism

The sangha was, in fact, the miniature model of socialism, where all could assemble without having any regard to high or low births.

The Buddha is stated to have reminded that just as the rivers lose their independent identities after merging with the ocean, similarly, the members of the four castes also lose their names and the membership of the various castes after joining the sangha, and subsequently they are known as bhikkhus, the sons of Sakyamuni or bhikkhunis (nuns).

Forget yourself, then you realise Buddhism

Zen master Dogen said, "To study Buddhism is to study yourself, to study yourself is to forget yourself, and to forget yourself is to perceive yourself as all things."

Then you come to know that the concept of self is an illusion.

The path to escape from disaster

The path that the Buddha showed us is, I believe, the only path humanity must tread if it is to escape disaster. For us it should be our peculiar good fortune to try to tread that path.

~ Pandit Nehru ~

What is most important for salvation?

- For Indian religionists,
  renunciation is important.
- For Chinese religionists,
  living in the society
  to cultivate virtues is important.
- To all the other religionists,
  God is important.
- For Buddhists,
  purification of the mind is the ultimate goal.

The noble ones do not appreciate evil

Having seen the danger in the world,
Having known the state without clinging,

A noble one does not delight in evil;
In evil a pure one finds no delight.

~ Buddha - Ud ~

The three eyes described by the Buddha

The fleshly eye, the divine eye,
And the unsurpassed wisdom eye —
These three eyes were described
By the Buddha, supreme among men.

The arising of the fleshly eye
Is the path to the divine eye,
But the unsurpassed wisdom eye
Is that from which knowledge arises.
By obtaining such an eye
One is released from all sufferings.

~ Buddha - It. V ~

Dharma quenches your thirst

Having drunk this Dharma medicine,
You will be ageless and beyond death;

Buddhism is the by-product of Dharma

Having developed and seen the truth,
You will be quenched, free from craving.

~ Buddha - Miln: 335 ~

Arahantas can exist anytime

As long as my disciples lead a pure,
religious life,
So long will the world never
become empty of Arahantas.

~ Buddha - Dig ~

Dharma exists forever

O Monks, whether there is the appearance
of Perfected Ones
Or there is not the appearance of Perfected Ones,
There is this established condition of Dharma,
This fixed law of Dharma.
All conditioned phenomena are impermanent,
sorrowful and not self
A perfected one who has fully awakened

Is one who fully understands.
He then declares, expounds, and explains that
All conditioned phenomena are impermanent,
sorrowful, and not self.

~ Buddha - A ~

Dharma is the highest gift

The gift of Dharma excels all gifts
The flavour of Dharma excels all flavours
The pleasure in Dharma excels all pleasures
He who has destroyed craving (*tanha*) over-
comes all sorrow.

~ Buddha - Dh. ~

Door to end death is opened!

The door to deathlessness is opened!
Let those who will hear leave wrong beliefs,
Now shall I turn the wheel
of the great Law (*Dharma*),
For this I go to the Kasian City
There shall I beat the drum of deathlessness,

Buddhism is the by-product of Dharma

In this world where people are groping
in the darkness (of ignorance).

~ Buddha - M ~

What is Nirvana?

The destruction of greed and lust (*lobha*),
The destruction of ill-will and hatred (*dosa*),
The destruction of delusion and ignorance (*moha*),
That friend, is called Nirvana.

~ Buddha - S ~

What Nirvana contributes

As the lotus is unstained by water,
So is Nirvana unstained by all the defilements.
As cool water allays feverish heat,
So also Nirvana is cool and
allays the fever of all passions.
As water quenches the thirst of men and
beasts who are
Exhausted, parched and overcome by heat,
So also Nirvana quenches the craving for

sensuous enjoyments, further being, and
cessation of being.
As medicine protects from the torments of poison,
So Nirvana from the torments of
poisonous passions.
As medicine puts an end to sickness,
and nourishes like nectar,
Nirvana ends all suffering and
nourishes by giving peace...

~ Buddha - M ~

Why I could not catch you

One day, the Buddha went to meet Angulimala, a murderer who terrorised the whole country. When Angulimala saw the Buddha, he was very happy because he could kill the last person to complete the number of people he needed to kill to fulfil his vow.

With sword in his hand, he ran at the Buddha to catch him. He ran and ran until he became very tired, but he still could not reach the Buddha. Finally he shouted to the Buddha, "Stop!"

The Buddha said, " I have already stopped long ago."
Angulimala said, "But you were walking."
The Buddha then said, "The meaning of 'stop' is that I have stopped committing evil deeds."
Then Angulimala asked, "Why, I could not catch you after running such a long distance?"
The Buddha replied, "You could not catch me because you ran. If you stop running, you can catch me!"
Angulimalia asked again, "What do you mean?"
The Buddha said, "The meaning of the word 'run' means you are committing evil deeds for you to suffer for a long time in your life."

Angulimala then decided to give up his cruel act of killing and followed the Buddha to become one of his disciples.

Albert Einstein on Buddhism

This is perhaps most clearly exemplified by the remark said to have been made by the great twentieth-century scientist Albert Einstein, that although he was not a religious man, if he had been one, he would have been a Buddhist.

~ The Tree of Enlightenment ~

Buddha is like a physician

The Buddha is like a physician. Just as a doctor must know the diagnosis of the different kinds of illness, their causes, the antidotes and remedies, and must be able to apply them, so also the Buddha has taught the Four Holy Truths which indicate the range of suffering, its origin, its cessation, and the way which lead to its cessation.

~ Dr. Edward Conze ~

5

Duty of a Religion

Our belief in some power beyond the world is as old as the human race. Different religions have given this belief enduring substance, and spawned a rich diversity of ritual and ceremony. While theologians debate religious truths, great philosophers attempt to understand our physical world, grappling with logic in their search for knowledge and certainty.

The word 'religion' has no one generally accepted definition. Philosophers, sociologists, psychologists, theologians and many others interested in a particular aspect of life, have all defined religion in their own ways and for their own purposes.

However, the main purpose of every religion is to teach people how to lead a respectable and harmless life and to find out their liberation from physical and mental suffering.

Religions are meant for the emancipation of living beings. Religions are not mere subjects of study and essay writing, but are practical modes of conduct in the grooming of human beings externally in matters of the mundane and internally in things that concern the inner spirit. Religion must be experienced at the very source of its beginning and lived in utter abandonment, through all phases of change to attain a spirituality and inner growth.

Among all the great founders of religions, it was the Buddha alone who encouraged the spirit of investigation among his followers. He advised them not to accept even his teachings with blind faith and without thorough impartial investigation. Therefore, it is no exaggeration to say that Buddhism can be called a religion of science. Whatever scientists have discovered so far, they has never gone against the teachings of the Buddha.

Buddhism is truly a religion suited to the modern, scientific world. The light, which comes from nature, from science, from history, from human experience, from every point of the universe, is radiant with the Noble Teachings of the Buddha.

Religion is a system of education

Religion is, among many other things, a system of education, by means of which human beings may train themselves, first to make desirable changes in their own personalities and in society, and, to heighten consciousness and so establish more adequate relations between themselves and the universe of which they are parts.

~ *Aldous Huxley* ~

A religion of freedom

The freedom that the followers of the Buddha enjoy is commendable. In fact, many Buddhists have not even realised this themselves. They have full freedom to judge and to think for themselves whether to accept or to reject anything.

They are not bound to accept anything in the name of religion, either simply by thinking of the greatness of a particular religious teacher, or, by thinking that it is their bounden duty to accept the words of holy scriptures, or, the ways of ancient traditions.

Buddhists are at liberty to investigate for themselves and accept or reject any proposition in accordance with their own conviction, based on reason.

Purpose of religion

Annihilation of all greed,
Extinction of all hatred,
Cessation of all ignorance.
Cultivation of virtue and wisdom.

Different aspects of religion

Personal Religion means the inward veneration of one's religious teacher or teachers and the application of one's moral principles in one's daily life, without participating in the showy manifestations of the organised religion of the masses. The intellectually liberated belong to this category.

Organised or Institutionalised Religion is the popularly practised religion of the masses, with much pomp, many ceremonies, processions and public worship. Temple festivals are typical examples of institutionalised religion.

Intellectuals are not very much interested in this kind of religion, but the broad masses are really interested in it.

Buddhism satisfies all religious needs: to the intellectual classes, it gives a lofty philosophy and moral teachings that lead to enlightenment and liberation from all sufferings; to the common person, it gives a focal point for worship and the hope of a better life hereafter.

Revealed Religion is said to be '*revealed*' by '*God*' through a prophet or special messenger of a God. Christianity, Judaism and Islam are regarded as revealed religions. Adherents of those religions, regard them as the only true religions.

They are monotheistic religions, believing in one God. Catholicism, however, has yielded to the popular and more natural demand for more gods, by introducing the belief in the intercession of the 'Mother of God' and their Saints, the worship or adoration of the relics of the Saints, and still many other ways of approaching God and obtaining what one wants without having to ask directly from the 'One God'.

Natural Religion the worship of natural phenomena and forces, is said to have been inspired by the aspect of Nature. The first form of natural religion might have been really inspired by the awe experienced in the presence of strong natural phenomena, such as sun, moon, mountains, rivers, sea, earthquakes, thunderstorms, floods, and any violent changes in one's environment.

It is fear and desire to win the favour of the powers behind the natural phenomena, which gave rise to the belief in gods, souls, spirits and mighty divine beings, and the possibility of incurring their displeasure or winning their favour.

Ancestor worship is a form of religion which leads to the worship of ancestors or the First Man, or a God, who is supposed to have been the originator of the imperial family and of all men. The Japanese and the Chinese, who are not considered as Buddhists or adherents of other systems are the adherents of this kind of religion.

Psychological Religion is occupied with the study of the nature of human soul and its relation to God. Though the Hindus declare that their religion is one revealed by God or successive incarnations of God, their religion is often described as a Psychological Religion that mixed with Natural Religion.

Buddhism as a religion

Buddhism is not a message or something revealed by a supernatural divine being. Buddhism is the Dharma or universal phenomena understood by the Buddha through his enlightenment. Dharma is to understand the nature of life and worldly conditions and to train oneself by leading a righteous way of life and also to gain mental tranquillity, wisdom and finally deliverance from physical and mental sufferings.

Buddhism and atheism

Though free thinkers and atheists at times, acclaim the Buddha as one of their own, yet Buddhism is not an Atheistic Teaching, if the word 'atheism' is used in a derogatory sense of reproach and condemnation. Buddhism does not waste time in fighting against belief in God or gods. When rightly understood, it supersedes all theistic as well as atheistic doctrines.

Humans without a religion are difficult to govern

A government cannot control human beings merely by imposing more and more rigid rules. The more the government makes rules, the more the people would find loopholes to break them. If man were morally trained by a religion which makes him understand why he should behave as a good citizen, no problems would arise.

Unlike human beings, animals have no politics or government, religion or education, but yet maintain themselves without facing many difficulties among themselves. What would be the situation among human beings, if they were allowed to live without any government, religion or education?

Allergy to other religions

To the followers of some religions, all other religions are to be avoided as if they are some contagious diseases.

By abusing another's religion one damages one's own religion

One should not honour only one's own religion and condemn the religions of others, but one should honour others' religions for this or that reason. In so doing, one helps one's own religion to grow and renders service to the religions of others too. In acting otherwise, one digs the grave of one's own religion and also does harm to other religions. Whosoever honours his own religion and condemns other religions, does so indeed through devotion to his own religion, thinking, "I will glorify my own religion." But on the contrary, in so doing he injures his own religion more gravely. So concord is good. Let all listen, and be willing to listen to the doctrines professed by others.

~ Emperor Asoka - Rock edict ~

Why some people regard the followers of other religions as their enemies

- Why is it that sometimes the followers of one religious group treat another religious group as rivals?
- Why are they reluctant to show their smiling faces to other religionists?
- Why are they sometimes hostile to others and why do they refuse even to co-operate with their good work?
- Why do some insult other religious people by

calling them names?

Such people must understand that the co-religionists are also working for human welfare and do not wish to harm or mislead the public.

There cannot be only one religion

Religionists must come together and work with each other. Mahatma Gandhi once said, "I do not expect the India of my dream to develop one religion, to be wholly Hindu, Christian or wholly Muslim, but I want it to be wholly tolerant with its religions working side by side with one another."

People may cheat the government but not religion

People may cheat the government but not religion. One who tries to cheat religion cheats oneself. Discipline cannot be brought out by coercion and compulsion or by science, but by sincerely following a religion, which stands for peace, purity and happiness.

The weakness of a religion cannot be inferred by observing what people practise

One should not judge the merits or demerits of a religion simply by watching certain ill-conceived practices and beliefs adopted by illiterate people in the name of religion.

The original teachings of the great teachers are open to everybody and must be examined before criticism is made.

How people misunderstand religion

Irreligion is sometimes propagated under the garment of religion. Many people think religion is to be found only in a place of worship and a guru. Many people regard religion as suitable for old folks or women but not for the youths, educated or rich people.

To them religion can only be found within the covers of some musty books but not among the flowers that bloom so freshly in the fields. These ideas are the results of their negligence, laziness and misunderstanding of religion.

No righteous anger in Buddhism

In Buddhism, there is no such thing as righteous indignation or righteous anger; Buddhism never tried to justify war under any circumstances. There was no nervous irritability or emotion or anger in the Buddha's mind just because some people did not pay attention to him.

Respect those who are worthy of respect

As Buddhists, we can respect and honour the founders and teachers of other religions. All religious teachers deserve respect and honour, for they also have done good service to mankind. If we like, we also can keep pictures or symbols of these religious teachers in our homes. Buddhism advises us to honour those who are worthy of honour.

Buddhism is a living religion

Buddhism influenced Indian life in a hundred ways, as it was bound to, for it must be remembered that it was a living, dynamic, and wide-spread religion in India for over a thousand years.

~ Pandit Nehru ~

Some religions encourage war

They say, war is an open door to heaven. Those who die in the battlefield for God will be born in heaven.

How to prove the progress of a religion?

We cannot show the progress of a religion simply by erecting big buildings as places of worship, or by making huge images, or through various functions and ceremonies, or organising some colourful and attractive religious activities to bring more and more people into religion.

But we can show the progress of a religion according to the behaviour of the followers of the religion, how they convince others through their decent life and kindness, sincerity, harmless and unblamable life.

Who is a religious man?

In the eyes of the Buddha, a religious man is one who is leading a noble life. Such a person can be a follower of any religion or even a person without any religious label.

Yet, if such a person could purify his mind from various defilements or evil thoughts, then he will be able to enjoy a happy, peaceful, contented life and finally attain everlasting happiness.

It is not easy for a person to prove that he is more religious than others, just because he worships and prays so many times a day or by making offerings in the name of a god or a religious teacher.

We believe that the only way to be religious is by following noble principles to develop the moral and spiritual aspects of our life without harming others.

Who is the sinner?

It is a sin to call a man a sinner.

Theistic and humanistic religion

Theistic religions worship supernatural powers. Humanistic religions worship human goodness. They say: Human virtues are more powerful than divine power. Buddhism recognises the divinity of humans and goodness within human nature.

The wise one sees only good things in every religion

Like the bee gathers honey from different flowers, the wise one sees only the good in all religions and accepts the essence of the different teachings.

For example:

- Buddhism says, "Hurt not others in ways that you yourself would find hurtful."
- Taoism says, "Regard your neighbour's gain as your own gain, and your neighbour's loss as your own loss."
- Christianity says, "All things whatsoever ye would that men should do to you, do ye even so to them."

- Islam says, "Do unto all men as you would they do unto you, and reject others that you would reject for yourself."
- Hinduism says, "Let no one do to others what he would not have done to himself."

Where religions originate

All the other religions begin in heaven and descend to earth, like the stalactite.

Buddhism begins on earth and ascends up to heaven, like the stalagmite.

Comparison between Buddhism and Christianity

- Christianity is theocentric, as it is centred around the concept of God; while Buddhism is anthropocentric, as it is centred around the concept of man.
- For the Christian, religion has come down from Heaven to earth to fulfil the purpose of the Creator; for the Buddhist, religion has grown

up on earth to fulfil a human need, to solve a human problem.

- For the Christian, man is the image of God in imperfect form, which God creates and attempts to perfect through the practice of religion; for the Buddhist, God is the image of man in perfect form, which man conceives and attempts to realise, through the practice of religion.
- For the Christian, Christ is God become man, the 'Anthropomorphic God'; for the Buddhist, the Buddha is man become God (Brahma bhuto), the 'Theopsychic Man'.
- For the Christian, the practice of religion is co-operation with God to satisfy his divine purpose; for the Buddhist, the practice of religion is the fulfilment of a human need to overcome evil, suffering and ignorance, by transcending human weakness.
- For the Christian, the practice is based on the belief in God and his plan; for the Buddhist, the practice is based on an understanding of the problem of human existence and its

solution through an inner transformation.

~ Rev. M. Punnaji ~

Religion and divine nature

The religious way of life is the cultivation of humane qualities and when life is purified it is called divine power. However, it is essential to maintain human dignity and also give credit to human intelligence.

Why religion is so important to man

Human beings do not know what to do
With their lives and how to use it properly.
Religion gives them the answer.
Life without religion is like a ship
Without anchor or navigator.

Why religious discrimination?

There is no religion in this world that encourages the followers of another religion to practise their own religion.

One religion is being used to discriminate against another religion and develop jealousy or hostility. It seems people are not using religion to maintain peace but to condemn and hate others. This unhealthy religious arrogance and competition have even created violence and bloodshed in many parts of the world.

At the same time, while cherishing their own imagination or concepts, which they regard as part of their culture or tradition, some religionists ridicule the culture and traditions of others. In their beliefs and practices, which are introduced as the only true religion, they promote such selfish ideas for material gain, political power and self-glorification.

Communism and religion

Some countries attempt to oust religion and introduce communism or socialism. Today their people are turning back to religion.

Science and religion

Science without religion is lame.
Religion without science is blind.

~ Albert Einstein ~

Theory and practice

Theory without practice is empty.
Practice without theory is blind.

Belief in charms and magic

Some people resort to charms, magic, supernatural powers and mantras to overcome their problems. But nobody knows just how far they can succeed through such beliefs and practices.

~ Swami Vivekananda ~

When ritualism arises

When the way of natural harmony is lost then virtue arises; after virtue is lost then justice arises; after justice is lost then ritualism arises.

~ Lao Tze ~

Duty of a Religion

Supernatural power

The idea of supernatural beings may arouse to a certain extent the power of the action in man but it also brings spiritual decay.

It brings dependence, fear and superstition. It degenerates into a horrible belief in the natural weakness of the man.

~ Swami Vivekananda ~

When religion is important

A man who puts aside his religion because he is very busy in society is like one taking off his shoes because he is about to walk upon thorns.

Political leaders and religion

Political leaders have no authority to impose religious laws.

Their duty is to uphold the religious principles introduced by the enlightened religious teachers to maintain peace and order in society.

Why some people do not like religion

Some people do not like religion because religion asks them not to do many things that they like to do and to do many things which they do not like to do.

Religious twists

The followers of many religions are twisting and turning religious teachings to conform to worldly needs. This is to satisfy their desires and to influence others' thinking by claiming that they are promoting religion. But they are not worried that this reinterpretation will lead them towards a dead end.

Religious principles should never be surrendered to satisfy the need for human gratification. Rather, religious principles should be upheld for human development.

Why religion was introduced

Religious belief is the invention of a wise

statesman who wished to restrain men from secret and hidden vices.

~ Critias, uncle of Plato ~

We do only window-shopping

If we neglect our intellectual ability and believe in rites, rituals, ceremonies and dogmas, we no longer seek the truth but engage in window-shopping.

Buddhism is for human needs

From the Buddhist point of view religion is not something that has come down from heaven to fulfil a divine purpose, but something that has grown up on earth to satisfy the deepest of human needs: peace, happiness and liberation.

What is a real religious way of life?

According to the Buddha, indulging in prayers, mantras, penances, hymns or songs, charms, incantations and invocations and animal sacrifices to please the gods, fasting to death, not taking medicines when sick, sleeping on hard ground, burning and cutting or poking of bodies as punishments for committing evil deeds or observing complete silence without talking are not the real religious practices to get rid of problems and suffering or to wash away the bad karma (sins) committed.

Only by leading a respectable, noble and harmless or blameless pure life, can one gain true salvation.

Develop harmony and understanding with others

The religious life can only be established when man is ready to accept responsibilities for himself and others, and not because of reward or punishment.

The purpose of religion is to help man to think correctly, to raise him above the level of the animal, to help him understand his relationship with the universe and to live in harmony with it so that he reaches his ultimate goal of supreme happiness and fulfilment.

Everything is interdependent

World depends on God and
God depends on world. All are interdependent.

~ Prof. Whitehead ~

Experience of the divine in man

Religion is not a set of doctrines but it is experience. And religious experience is based on the realisation of the presence of the divine in man.

~ Dr. Radhakrishnan ~

Hunting grounds for missionaries

Ignorance and poverty are very successful hunting grounds for missionaries.

God must be in the mind

Beware of the man
whose god is in the skies.

~ George Bernard Shaw ~

How we behave in front of God

Before God we are all equally wise —
equally foolish.

~ Albert Einstein ~

Why religion influences hatred

We have just enough religion to make us hate,
but not enough to make us love one another.

~ Jonathan Swift ~

Religion is to conquer

Religion is the conquest of fear;
the antidote of failure and death.

~ Dr. Radhakrishnan ~

Duty of a Religion

Moral conduct and religion

Religion is the central part of our education that determines our moral conduct.

~ H. G. Wells ~

Moral principles are in religion

Religion is the recognition of our moral principles as laws that must not be transgressed.

~ Kant ~

Concept of god is important

If the concept of god did not exist, somehow or other, man would have created one because it is very important for his psyche. A divine power is necessary to allay our innate fear.

~ Anatole France ~

The origin of religion

When the concept of God or divinity was imbued into the human mind, religion sprang up in the world.

Who should punish an offender?

When Jesus Christ met a group of people who were about to stone a woman to death for misbehaviour, he said, "Let him who is without sin cast the first stone."

Religion and materialism

The main reason why materialism has grown to be so powerful and influential in the modern world is because science has proven that many of those concepts maintained as religious beliefs are unacceptable.

Therefore, there are very few educated and intelligent people who can wholeheartedly subscribe to such beliefs. Some people still uphold them but only as part of their traditions or culture.

On the other hand, some people modify these concepts by using their common sense and give new interpretations to age-old practices.

The things that science cannot do

Today, so many people are plagued with fear, restlessness, and insecurity. Yet science fails to rescue them. Science is unable to teach the common man to control his mind when he is driven by the animal nature that burns within him.

Science is unable to provide a meaningful plan and purpose for life. It cannot provide man a clear reason for his living. In fact, science is thoroughly secular in nature and unconcerned with man's spiritual goal.

The danger of science without religion

Without having moral ideals, science poses a danger to all mankind. Science has made the machine which in turn gains control.

The bullet and bomb are gifts of science to the few in power on whom the destiny of the world depends. Meanwhile the rest of mankind waits in anguish and fear.

Duty of science and religion

Science asks what the world is and religion asks what mankind and society should become.

~ Albert Einstein ~

The duty of philosophy and religion

Philosophy is to understand
the nature of the world.
Religion is to understand
the worldly conditions and
to live according to such conditions.

The aim of philosophy

To a Greek, philosophy is to make man wise
To a Chinese, philosophy is to make man virtuous
To an Indian, philosophy is to seek release.

Religions are not all the same

In spite of some similarities amongst religions, it is intellectual hypocrisy or a well-meaning lie, to say all religions are the same. It would be more correct to say that the *aim* of all religions is the same; that is, to find peace, eternal bliss or salvation. But the methods adopted to achieve that aim by various religions are not the same and some may even be controversial.

Cows are of many colours but the colour of the milk is always the same. Therefore the aim of religion is the same as the colour of milk.

Buddhism is for brotherhood

It was not to be an organisation for converting those of other faiths, but a brotherhood of mind and heart ready to help those, who had been inspired by the teachings of the Buddha and who wanted to put it into practice as human beings.

~ Anagarika Govinda ~

Humanistic religion

The Buddha Dharma is humanistic in its basis.

It is not a teaching about ghosts (spirits) or gods.

~ Ven. Yin Sun ~

Conversion is meaningless

For inward satisfaction and growth, people change their religions. I am against modern methods of conversion that people perform as if doing some business.

~ Mahatma Gandhi ~

Purpose of religious education

The main purpose of religious education today is not to impose our thoughts and way of life on others, not to replace one religion with another, but to discover what others are doing, and to help them live their lives peacefully.

~ Dr. Radhakrishanan ~

Faith

You can do very little with faith,
but you can do nothing without it.

~ Samuel Butler ~

Duty of a Religion

Education can produce clever devils

If education is given without proper religious guidance, we make the young but clever devils. If man is selfish and wicked even with religion, what would he be without a religion?

Let all religionists unite for peaceful survival

- Let all religionists unite not to use religious militarism.
- Let them unite to stop all brutality and manslaughter in the name of war.
- Let them unite to give freedom to man to find a religion according to his own conviction.
- Let them unite to give up religious monopoly.
- Let them unite not to use religion in the market-place to convert others by adopting questionable methods.
- Let them unite to respect the other man's religious beliefs and practices as long as these beliefs and

practices are harmless and do not mislead the public.

- Let them unite to wipe out the challenging attitude of unhealthy religious competition.
- Let all religionists unite to eliminate the various vices and immoral practices that are common in our modern society.
- Let them also unite to introduce the moderate way of life amongst their followers and advise them not to go to extremes.

The religion of the future

If there were any religion that would cope with modern scientific needs it would be Buddhism. Buddhism has the characteristics of what would be expected in a cosmic religion for the future: It transcends a personal god, avoids dogmas and theology; it covers both the natural and the spiritual, and it is based on a religious sense arising from the experience of all things, natural and spiritual, as a meaningful unity.

~ Albert Einstein ~

Duty of a Religion

Pastor and taxi driver in heaven

One day, a pastor travelling in a taxi realised that the driver was driving recklessly. The pastor became worried about his safety and kept praying to God. But the stubborn driver continued to drive recklessly and thereby caused an accident. As a result, both of them died on the spot. They had the opportunity to go to heaven. However, when they reached heaven the pastor was stopped by the person in charge and was asked to wait outside. The taxi driver instead was warmly welcomed.

This caused the pastor to become angry and he argued, "It is very unfair. I have been preaching about God for a long time, whereas this taxi driver had never worked for God. How can he enter heaven before me?" To this, the person in charge explained, "Yes, we know that, but what we wish to evaluate is the outcome. When you were preaching, the congregation lost interest and fell asleep. But in the case of the taxi driver, he encouraged all his passengers to remember God and to pray whilst he was driving. Thus, he has earned more credit than you."

To me, hell is better than heaven

I prefer to go to hell rather than heaven. I believe heaven is good for playboys but not for me. Many of those intellectuals like the scientists, great thinkers, rationalists including the Buddha are in hell because they did not believe in God. So if I go to hell I will have a nice time with them.

~ R. Ingersoll ~

The time when God takes a rest

People doubt if God indeed has enough time to rest or sleep, because he has to keep a constant eye on them to see if they are up to create violence or not.

Some people say that when they pray to God, that would be the time he could take the opportunity to relax, knowing that people have no chance to create violence while praying.

Duty of a Religion

Only one religion

There is only one religion,
though there are a hundred versions of it.

~ George Bernard Shaw ~

Difficulty for a rich man to enter heaven

It is easier for a camel to go through the eye of a needle than for a rich man to enter heaven.

~ Jesus Christ ~

God listen to the heart

God is not interested in what the mouth says.
He is interested in what the heart says.

~ Vision ~

Do not cling to view

O Bhikkhus, even this view — Dharma
Which is so pure and so clear,
If you cling to it, if you fondle it,
If you are attached to it,
Then you do not understand,

That the teaching is similar to a raft,
Which is for crossing over and
Not for getting hold of.

~ Buddha - M ~

Belief in permanent soul

Monks, if there is a theory of permanent soul, grasping to which does not bring about grief, suffering, anguish, lamentation and despair, grasp onto it. But monks, do you see such a theory of soul?

~ Buddha - M ~

No religious monopoly on truth

No one religion, no matter how superior it is considered to be, has a monopoly on truth. Nor is any one religion the perfect embodiment of truth.

Given this fact, it would be best if different religions of the world would cooperate and support each other.

Duty of a Religion

Real holy man

A holy man is one who never considers himself superior to any single creature on earth and who has renounced all the pleasures of life.

~ Mahatma Gandhi ~

God's power

God's great power is in the gentle breeze,
not the storm.

~ Dr. Rabindranath Tagore ~

Who is the real holy man?

- Whosoever does no harm to living creatures.
- Whosoever does not kill or
  participate in killing,
  is to be called a holy man.
- Whosoever is tolerant with the intolerant.
- Whosoever patiently tolerates punishment.
- Whosoever shows compassion to all cretures,
  is to be called a holy man.

~ Buddha – Ud ~

A great man has nothing to claim

Foxes have dens, and birds of the sky have nests, but the son of man has nowhere to lay his head.

~ Jesus Christ ~

Joyful religion

Buddhism is quite opposed to the melancholic, sorrowful, penitent and gloomy attitude of mind, which is considered a hindrance to the realisation of Truth.

On the other hand, it is interesting to remember here that joy is one of the seven 'Factors of Illumination', the essential qualities to be cultivated for the realisation of Nirvana.

~ Ven. Dr. W. Rahula ~

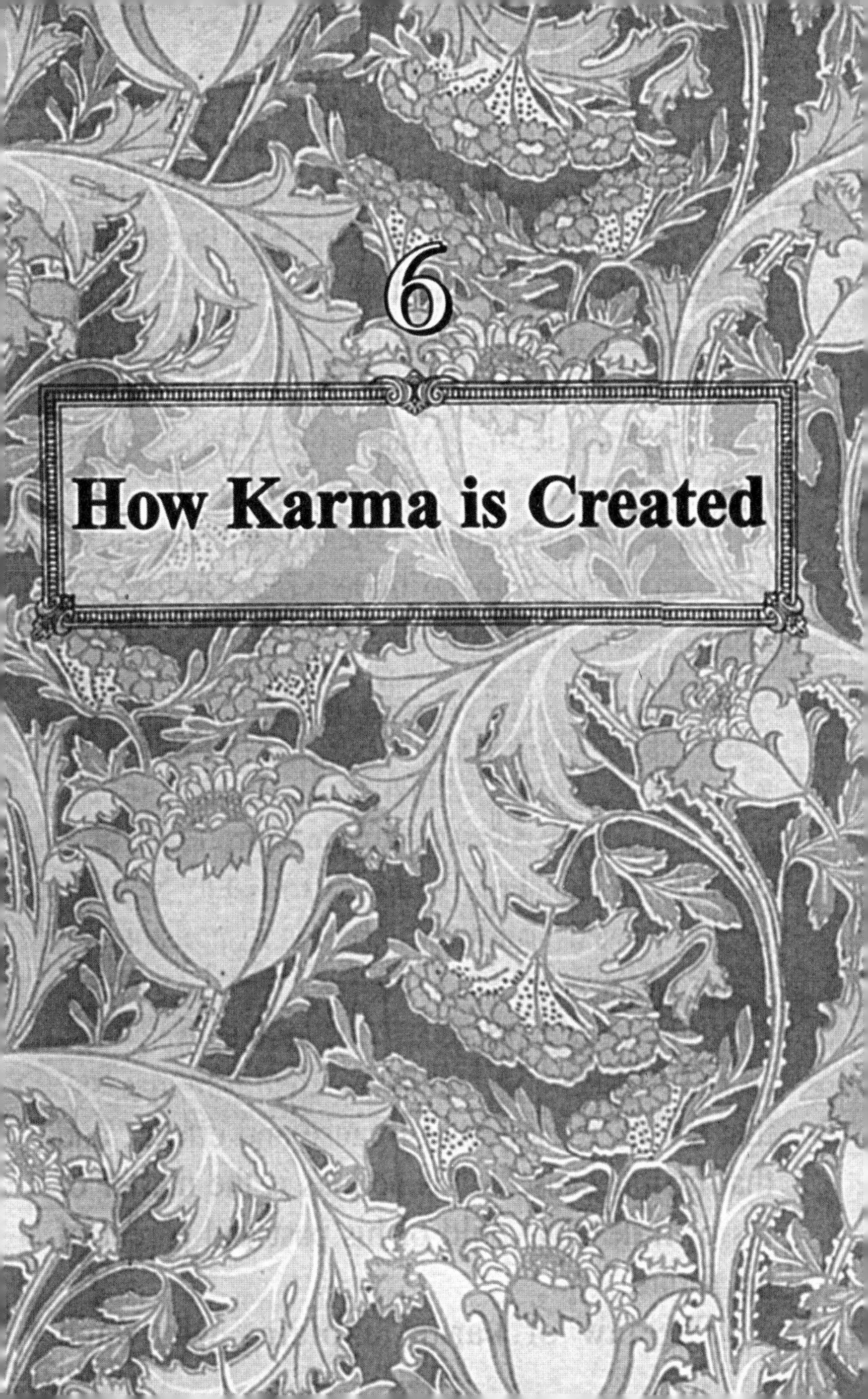

6

How Karma is Created

arma (*Sanskrit*) and Kamma (*Pali*) is the principle that all good and bad actions have consequences that will affect one throughout life, and even in future lives. By extension, karma is sometimes loosely used to mean fate, or destiny. Man is the architect of his own fate, and he will reap what he sows.

Thus, the material and mental forces combine and recombine with no underlying substance or soul to make them permanent, and this process of becoming, the wheel of life, continues indefinitely unless its cause, craving or selfish desire for existence, is totally extinguished. It is this desire, which sets the wheel of life in motion, and it is manifested in action, which is in reality volition or will-power. Volitional action is responsible for the creation of a being.

Every action produces an effect; cause comes first and effect afterwards. We therefore may say that karma is the 'law of cause and effect', and that man because of his actions is the master of his own destiny, child of his past and parent of his future.

The law of karma explains why each

individual has a unique mental disposition, a unique physical appearance and unique response to experiences. These are the various effects of the countless actions that each individual had performed in the past and which are stored as mental habits.

At the root of man's trouble is his primal state of ignorance, and from ignorance arises desire, which sets the karmic force in motion. According to the law of karma, the tragedy of inequality in creation itself, falls short of any reasonableness. For instance the sadness of the spastic child and the sadness of the deaf and dumb, cannot easily be accommodated in the concept of a Compassionate Creator.

The Law of Cause and Effect is a logical and a reasonable explanation of the tragedy that is creation itself. The universal law of karma throws a challenge and helps one to become the means to control one's own fate.

Just as the law of this country does not make exceptions for certain categories of people so the law of karma does not exclude people on account of their intellect or other characteristics.

Karma and rebirth account for many of our existing problems

- They account for the suffering for which we ourselves are responsible.
- They explain the inequality of mankind.
- They account for the arising of geniuses and child prodigies.
- They explain why identical twins who are physically alike, enjoying equal privileges, exhibit totally different characteristics, mentally, intellectually and morally.
- They account for the dissimilarities amongst children of the same family although heredity may account for the similarities.
- They account for special abilities of men by their parental tendencies.
- They account for the normal and intellectual differences between parents and children.
- They explain how infants spontaneously develop such passions as greed, anger and jealousy.
- They account for instinctive likes and dislikes at first sight.

How Karma is Created

- They explain how in us is found 'a rubbish heap of evil and treasure of good'.
- They account for the unexpected outbursts of passion in a highly civilised person, and for the sudden transformation of a criminal into a saint.
- They explain how profligates are born to saintly parents and saintly children to profligates.
- They explain how we are the result of what we were, we will be the result of what we are; in other words, we are not absolutely what we were, and will not be absolutely what we are.
- They explain the causes of untimely deaths, and unexpected changes in fortune.
- Above all, they account for the arising of omniscient, perfect spiritual teachers like the Buddhas who possess incomparable physical, mental and intellectual characteristics, which can be explained only by karma and rebirth.

~ Ven. Narada ~

We have to face the consequences of what we have done

If you fear pain, if you dislike pain,
Do not do a bad deed openly or in secret.
If you have done a bad deed or do one now,
You will not escape pain, though you try to flee.

~ Buddha - Ud ~

A single life is not enough to prepare for one's salvation

"If a single life here decides the whole course of the future, then why does one life last only for a few weeks, and another for 70 or 80 years?"

For one thing, the person who lives only a few weeks, risks less chance of eternal damnation than does the person who lives up to 80 years. The person who lives only a few weeks cannot fully develop and mature his intelligence and understanding. He does not encounter all the pitfalls and the temptations that life abounds with.

Karma and the electric light

Just as an electric light is the outward manifestation of invisible electric energy, even so are living beings the outward manifestation of invisible karmic energy. The bulb may break and the light may be extinguished, but the current remains and the light may be reproduced in another bulb. The bulb can be compared to the parental cell of the body and the electric energy to the karmic energy.

In the same way, the karmic force remains undisturbed by the disintegration of the physical body, and the passing away of the present consciousness leads to the arising of a fresh one in another birth.

Karma has neither beginning nor end

If we understand karma as a force or a form of energy, then we can discern no beginning. To ask where is the beginning of karma is like asking where is the beginning of electricity. Karma like electricity does not 'begin'. It 'comes into being' under certain conditions.

Conventionally, we say that the origin of karma is volition but this is as much conventional as saying that the origin of a river is a mountain top. But when you attain enlightenment, your karma exhausts (*kammakkhaya*). Therefore an individual's karma has no beginning but it has an end.

Three premonitory visions of the dying man

Suppose a person is about to die. This critical stage may be compared to the flickering of a lamp just before it is extinguished. To this dying man, the present karma or some good or bad actions committed either during his lifetime or immediately before his dying moment may cause a *karma nimitta* or *gati nimitta* to appear in the mind of the dying man.

Karma nimitta is a symbol or a mental reproduction of any sight, sound, smell, taste, touch or idea, which dominated his activity during his lifetime. Thus a butcher may see a vision of knives or dying animals. A kind physician may see his patients coming to him. A devotee may see an object of worship, etc.

A *gati nimitta* is a 'symbol of destiny' or a sign of the place where the rebirth is to occur. Such a symbol frequently presents itself to the dying person. Such premonitory visions of destiny may take various forms such as a fire, forests, mountainous regions, a mother's womb, celestial mansions, etc. When these indications of the future birth occur, and if they are bad, they might at times be remedied.

Rebirth takes place immediately irrespective of the place of birth, just as an electro-magnetic wave that is projected into space is immediately reproduced in a receiving radio set. Rebirth of the mental flux is also instantaneous and leaves no room whatever for any intermediate state (*antarabhava*).

The Buddha-word does not support the belief that a spirit of the deceased person takes lodgement in some temporary state until it finds a suitable place for its birth. According to certain beliefs there is an intermediate state where beings remain for one to seven weeks until the forty-ninth day. This view is contrary to the teachings of the Buddha.

Those who remember their previous births

Some people remember their previous births, but many others are unable to do so especially the following persons:

- Children who die young.
- Those who die old and senile.
- Those who are strongly addicted to drugs or intoxicants.
- Those whose mothers,
  during conception, have been sickly or
  have had to toil laboriously,
  or have been reckless
  or imprudent during pregnancy
- The foetuses in the womb,
  being stunned and startled,
  lose all knowledge of their past existence.

Cause and effect
instead of rewards and punishments

Buddhists believe in a just rationale of karma that operates automatically and speaks in terms of cause and effect instead of rewards and punishments.

Intentional actions create karma

Monks, I say that intention is karma.
When one intends, one acts by deed,
Word or thought.

~ Buddha - A. II: 82 ~

The purpose of explaining karma

The Buddhist doctrine of karma did not expound fatalistic views. Nor did it vindicate a post-mortem justice.

The Buddha, who had no selfish motives, did not teach this law of karma to protect the rich and comfort the poor by promising illusory happiness in an after-life.

~ Ven. Narada ~

Aspiration through merits

* Meritorious deed
  done for worldly pleasure is low.
* Meritorious deed
  done for one's own salvation is normal.
* Meritorious deed
  done for the well being of others is highest.

The law of causation

Buddhism teaches that consciousness is not a property of matter and life, is not a mere result of change produced by chemical or electric forces, but is a result of the Law of Causation.

One is responsible for one's own karma

My good man, it was through ignorance that
You did not act nobly in deed, word and thought.
That evil action of yours was
Not done by mother, father, brother, sister,
Friends and comrades.
Not by kinsmen, devas, recluses and Brahmins.

By yourself alone it was done.
It is just you that will experience
the fruit thereof.

~ Buddha - A. I: 138 ~

Bad effects come later

When a person is committing evil deeds
he feels it is sweet like honey.
Later when bad effects come,
he suffers like burning in the fire.

~ Buddha - Dh. ~

Only effects of good and bad deeds follow us

All our material properties remain behind when we depart from this world. Our relatives and friends follow us up to the graveyard only.

Only the good and bad actions (karma) that we have committed during our lifetime follow us into the next life either to support us or to disturb us.

What follows us after our death?

Germs, bacteria and viruses of the physical body never go with our body when we die.

However the germs such as greed, hatred and ignorance that we have harboured in our mind never remain behind but follow with our consciousness even after death.

A tree is known by its fruit

A good tree does not bear rotten fruit;
A rotten tree does not bear good fruit.
Are figs gathered from thorns,
or grapes from thistles?
Every tree is known by its fruit.

~ Jesus Christ ~

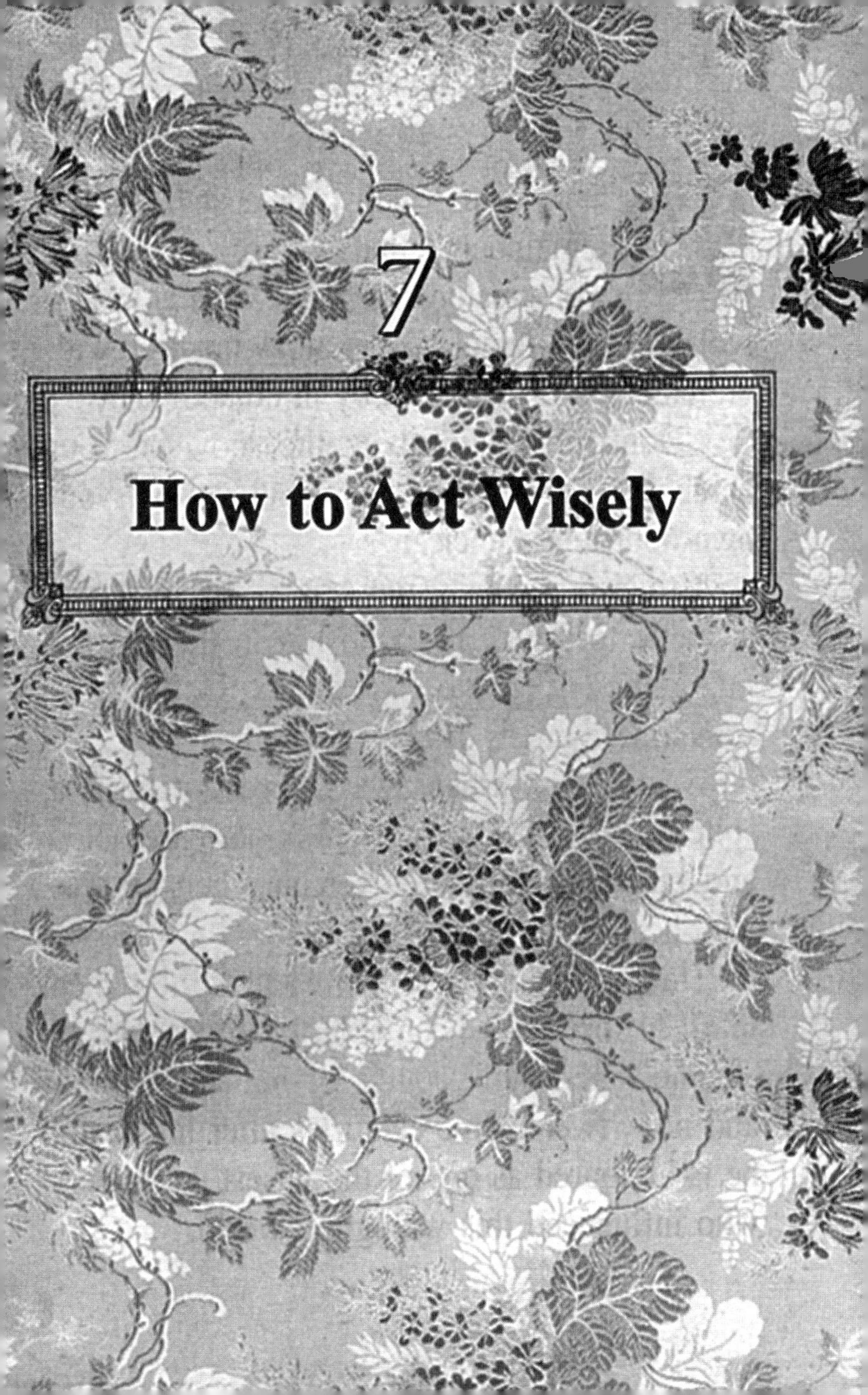

7

How to Act Wisely

When dealing with people, it has to be remembered that we are not dealing with creatures of logic. We are dealing with people of emotion, creatures bristling with prejudices and motivated by pride and vanity.

"Don't complain about the snow on your neighbour's roof," said Confucius, "when your own doorstep is unclean."

Criticism is a dangerous spark — a spark that is liable to ignite an explosion in the powder magazine of pride — an explosion that sometimes hastens death.

Socrates of Athens was a brilliant man in spite of the fact that he went about barefooted and married a girl of nineteen when he was bald-headed and forty.

He did something that only a handful of men in all history have been able to do; he sharply changed the whole course of human thought; and now, twenty-five centuries after his death, he is honoured as one of the wisest persuaders who influenced this wrangling world.

His method? Did he tell people they were wrong? Oh no, not Socrates. He was far too adroit for that. His whole technique, now called the 'Socratic method', was based upon getting a 'yes, yes' response. He asked questions with which his opponents would have to agree. He kept on winning one admission after another until he had an armful of 'yeses'. He kept on asking questions until finally, almost without realising it, his opponent found himself embracing a conclusion that he would have bitterly denied a few minutes previously. The next time we are smarting to tell a man he is wrong, let us remember barefooted old Socrates and ask a gentle question — a question that will get the 'yes, yes' response.

The Chinese have a proverb with the age-old wisdom of the changeless east: "He who treads softly goes far." They have spent five thousand years studying human nature, and they have treasured a lot of perspicacity: "He who treads softly goes far."

How they allocated charity box collections

Three groups of religious authorities, belonging to different religions, were discussing the ways on how to allocate their charity box collections at their respective places of worship.

The first group said that after opening the charity box they would draw a circle on the ground and toss the money upwards. Only money falling within the circle would be considered as belonging to God, and that falling outside would be used for other commitments.

The second group said their method was to draw a line on the ground and toss the money upwards. Money falling to the right side of the line would be considered as money belonging to God. The money falling on the left side of the line would be used for other activities.

The third group said the methods of the two earlier groups were not reliable as they can twist their hands so that more money would drop on their side.

According to their method the money is thrown upwards reached heaven belong to God and whatever falling on the ground would be theirs!

We have yet to learn the simple act

We have flown in the air like birds and have swum the sea like fishes, but we have yet to learn the simple act of walking on the earth like brothers and sisters.

~ Martin Luther King ~

Try to be good with confidence

There are no stars, which we could trust,
There is no guiding light,
And we know that we must
Be Good, Be Just, Be Right.

Keep life simple

We live and work and dream,
Each has his little scheme,
Sometimes we laugh;

Sometimes we cry,
And thus the days go by.

What is difficult to do?

- For the good to do what is good is easy,
- For the bad to do what is good is difficult;
- For the bad to do what is bad is easy,
- For the noble to do what is bad is difficult.

~ Buddha - Ud ~

Worthy of righteous life

Blessed are they who earn their living
without harming others.

~ Buddha ~

Do not cling too much

Say not that this is yours and that is mine,
Just say, this came to you and that to me,
So we may not regret the fading shine,
Of all the glorious things which cease to be.

In every good action there must be some sacrifice

No great work can be done without sacrifice.

~ Swami Vivekananda ~

Your own effort is better

What you discover on your own is always more exciting than what someone else discovers for you — it is like the difference between romantic love and an arranged marriage.

~ Terrence Rafferty ~

Humility leads to greatness

The tree laden with fruits always bend low.
So if you wish to be great be lowly and meek.

~ Sri Ramakrishna ~

Where is holiness?

The branches that bear most hang lowest
There is no true holiness without humility

Simplicity of a leader

Mahatma Gandhi, a leader of India always travelled third-class in a train.

Somebody once asked, "You are a leader of this country, why do you travel hird-class?" Mahatma Gandhi's reply was, "I travel third-class because there is no fourth-class."

Reflect before acting

"What think you, Rahula? What is a mirror for?"

"To reflect, Sir."

"In just the same way you must reflect again and again before doing every act. in speaking every word and in thinking every thought.

When you want to do anything you must reflect whether it would conduce to you or others' harm or both, and if so it is a wrong act, productive of woe and ripening unto woe.

If reflection tells you this is the nature of that contemplated fact, assuredly you should not do it. But if reflection assures you there is no harm but good in it, then you may do it."

~ Buddha - M. I: 415 ~

Be good yourself first

Let one first establish oneself
in what is proper, and then instruct others.
Such a wise man will not be blamed by others.

~ Buddha - Dh. 158 ~

Make life less difficult

What do we live for if it is not to make life less difficult for each other?

~ George Elliot ~

The danger of exploiting nature

The more we exploit nature,
The more our options are reduced,
Until we have only one —
To fight for our survival.

Shame and fear govern humanity

Shame to commit immoral deeds and
Fear of committing evil deeds.

~ Buddha ~

Don't cling to your own views

Some recluses and brahmins, so called,
Are deeply attached to their own views;
People who see only one side of things
Engage in quarrels and disputes.

~ Buddha - Ud ~

Different motivations of people

- One who works for his own good, but not for the good of others;
- One who works for the good of others, but not for his own good;
- One who works neither for his own good nor for the good of others;
- One who works for his own good as well as for the good of others.

~ Buddha ~

How to Act Wisely

Consider whether you are right

Do not just be concerned about your rights,
but consider whether or not you are right.

What is the secret of happiness?

The secret of happiness is not in doing
what one likes, but in liking what one does.

~ J. M. Barrie ~

You cannot find time but you can make it

You will never 'find' time for anything.
If you want it you can make it.

~ Charles Buxton ~

What can you take away from here?

He who holds his own self dear,
With evil let him not be linked.
An evil-doer's (short-lived) joy
Is not a bargain that is good.

Assaulted by the 'ender' death,
And losing his humanity,
What use for him is property
And what can he then take away?
What is it that will follow him?
Like his own shadow never parting?

Both the good and evil deeds
Which a mortal here performs,
These are his property indeed
That he will take away with him.
His deeds will follow after him
Like his own shadow never parting.
Hence noble deeds should be performed,
A store for the future life.
Good deeds will in the world beyond
Bestow on beings goodly help.

~ Buddha - A. III. I: 4 ~

Do one thing at a time

The surest way to do many things
is to do only one thing at a time.

Man develops himself

Everything that man has done for the upliftment of humanity has been done by man himself. Man's improvement must come from his own effort.

Only the wise cross the bridge

Those who have made a bridge
Cross over the river flood,
Leaving the swampy pools behind,
While people are binding a raft
The wise are already across.

~ Buddha - Ud ~

Man is not ready-made

Man today is the result of millions of past thoughts and actions. He is not ready-made but is always in the state of becoming. His own thinking process determines his character. Man is not perfect by nature; he has to train himself to be perfect. Man is not what he is, man is what he is not. That means: Human beings do not behave today as they should behave.

The angry man cannot see properly
When an angry man opens his mouth
he naturally closes his eyes.

The danger of ignoring others' evil deeds
The world is too dangerous to live in,
not because of people who do evil,
but because of people who sit and let it happen.

~ Albert Einstein ~

Only the wise experience heavenly bliss
If a person possesses these two things —
Good behaviour and a good view —
When his body perishes
That wise one is reborn in heaven.

~ Buddha - It. ~

Why cover only half of the body?
When Mahatma Gandhi visited England, some people asked him, "Why do you cover only half of your body.

Mahatma Gandhi replied, "The textile production in our country, when we distribute equally, I get only this much as my share."

Not knowing the meaning of his dress, people have nicknamed him as half-naked 'fakir' (beggar).

You cannot please all

Please all and you please none.

Practice is more important than theories

An ounce of practice is worth more than
a ton of theory.

~ E. F. Schumacher ~

Eat mindfully

When you eat, eat slowly and listen to your body. Let your stomach tell you when to stop not your eyes or your tongue.

~ Jack Kornfield ~

Difficult to get out
A habit is like a soft bed easy to get into,
but hard to get out of.

Greed loses more than gains
Greedy people always lose more than they gain.

Everybody means nobody
There was an important job to be done
And everybody was sure that
Somebody would do it;
Anybody could have done it
But nobody did it.

Somebody got angry with that
Because it was everybody's job.
But nobody realised that
Everybody wouldn't do it.

It ended up that everybody blamed
Somebody when nobody did what
Anybody could have done.

Criteria of right and wrong

No action is right simply because it is commended and no action is wrong simply because it is condemned.

The giver receives honour

No person was ever honoured for what he received: honour has been the reward for what he gave.

Cause and effect

He who sows evil reaps remorse.

~ Arabic proverb ~

Cause creates effect naturally

There is a suitable reward for every virtue and appropriate punishment for every sin a man commits. Both the reward and the punishment are effects over which no man has control, as they come upon him involuntarily.

~ Napoleon Hill ~

Learning how to give, not to regret

Learn how to give without hesitation, how to lose without regret, and how to acquire without meanness.

~ G. Sand ~

Your own feeling indicates that something is wrong with you

Blame, accusation, criticism and insults are unpleasant and painful but many point out our mistakes and weaknesses for us to think over to correct them. Therefore we should not hate those who criticise us. When we have physical pain, headache, cough and fever, such unpleasant feelings also create pain but they are not sicknesses.

Such painful feelings merely indicate to us that something is wrong somewhere in our body and give us warning to take precautions if we want to lead a healthy life. Therefore, it is meaningless to hate such unpleasant feelings but regard them as our friends.

Progress depends on not repeating the past

If we are to make progress,
we must not repeat history but make new history.

~ Mahatma Gandhi ~

Gods need salvation too

For the first time in human history, the Buddha admonished, entreated and appealed to people not to hurt a living being, and it is not necessary to offer prayer, praise or sacrifice to gods. With all the eloquence at his command the Buddha vehemently proclaimed that gods are also in dire need of salvation themselves.

~ Prof. Rhys Davids ~

Five kinds of trades not advisable for Buddhists

Trade in weapons, trade in human beings, trade in flesh (*breeding and selling animals for slaughter*), trade in liquor and trade in poisons.

Do not influence others about what you disbelieve

You cannot afford to suggest to another person,
by word of mouth or by an act of yours,
that which you do not believe.

~ Napoleon Hill ~

Never too late!

It is never too late to be
what you might have been.

~ George Eliot ~

What makes history?

The prophets of spirit make history
just by standing outside history.

~ Dr. Radhakrishnan ~

Love the truth and live it

- Those who know the truth learn to love it.
- Those who love the truth learn to live it.

Four courses of action

- Those who go from darkness to darkness — While leading a miserable life they commit more evil.
- Those who go from light to darkness — While enjoying pleasurable lives due to previous good karma they commit evil deeds.
- Those who go from darkness to light — Knowing that they are suffering in this life for their previous bad karma, they try to cultivate. Nobility in their lives for their future happiness.
- And those who go from light to light — While experiencing a pleasurable life, do more meritorious deeds to gain more happiness In their future lives.

~ Buddha - S. I. : 93 ~

Concentrate only on conditions

All things then depend on something else
On this depends the fact
that none are independent

Knowing this, we will not be annoyed at objects
That resemble magical appearance.
Thus when enemies or pleasant friends
Are seen to act improperly,
Be serene and tell yourself,
This comes from such and such conditions.

~ Shantideva ~

Humility is the foundation

Humility is the solid foundation of all virtues.

~ Confucius ~

How to help the poor?

The best thing you can do for the poor
is not to be one of them.

Effects of our actions are never lost

The effects of our actions may be postponed but
they are never lost. Thre is an inevitable reward

for good deeds and an inescapable punishment for bad. Meditate upon this truth and seek always to earn good wages from destiny.

~ Wu Ming Fu ~

'Impossible' is a fool's word

'Impossible' is a word only to be found
in the dictionary of fools.

~ Napoleon Bonaparte ~

Treat others like yourself

The rule for individual behaviour is —
What you do not want others to do to you,
Do not do them yourself.

~ Confucius ~

Excellence is a habit

We are what we repeatedly do;
Excellence, then, is not an act, but a habit.

~ Aristotle ~

Who is the best?

- The man who learns something from every man is wise.
- The man who overcomes his passion is strong.
- The man who is content with his fate is rich.
- The man who honours his fellow men is honoured.

~ Jewish saying ~

How to win

Proud looks lose hearts but courteous words win them.

How to make a life

We make a living by what we get, but we make a life by what we give.

~ Winston Churchill ~

What is ethics?

Ethics is the maintaining of life at the highest point of development.

~ Albert Schweitzer ~

How to Act Wisely

You weep alone

Laugh, and the world laughs with you.
Weep and you weep alone.

~ Shakespeare ~

Listen to yourself

Nobody can give you wiser advice
than yourself;
You will never err if you listen to
your own suggestions.

~ Cicero ~

Be realistic

Do what you can, with what you have,
where you are.

~ Theodore Roosevelt ~

Reason

Reason governs the wise man and
cudgels the fool.

Optimist and pessimist
An optimist laughs to forget;
a pessimist forgets to laugh.

Avoiding temptation
Don't worry about avoiding temptation.
As you grow wiser it will avoid you.

Do not try to fool others
You can fool some of the people all the time and all the people some of the time,
but you can't fool all the people all the time.

~ Abraham Lincoln ~

Putting off work
If you want to make an easy job seem mighty hard, just keep putting off doing it.

~ Olin Miller ~

Let go

Learn to let go.
That is the key to happiness.

~ Jack Kornfield ~

No proper date

One of these days is none of these days.

~ Henry George Bohn ~

Love your neighbours mindfully

Love your neighbours,
but don't pull down the fence.

~ Chinese proverb ~

Listen to your enemies

Pay attention to your enemies,
for they are the first to discover your mistakes.

Associate with the wise

Associate yourself with men of good quality
if you esteem your own reputation;
for it is better to be alone
than in bad company.

~ George Washington ~

The son who shines like the moon

The wise wish for a son
Who is superior or similar.
They do not wish for an inferior son —
One who disgraces the family.

But such sons in the world
Who are devoted lay followers,
Excelling in faith and virtue,
Liberal, without selfishness,
Shine forth in assemblies
Like the moon freed from clouds.

~ Buddha - It ~

Two things to forget

There are two things you must forget —
the good you do to others and
the wrong others do to you.

~ Sai Baba ~

Method of Lao Tze

Acting without design, occupying oneself without making a business of it, finding the great in what is small and the many in the few, repaying injury with kindness, effecting difficult things while they are easy, and managing great things in their beginnings; this is the method of Tao.

~ Lao Tze ~

When you protect others, you protect yourself

The greatest protection is a loving heart. Protecting yourself, you protect others. Protecting others, you protect yourself. (*Follow the red traffic light!*)

~ Jack Kornfield ~

Serve those who need

- If your speech has no sweetness,
  can your love be true?
- If you find fault with others,
  are you faultless and true?
- If one comes forward, will you go forward?
  To serve those who need you and
  God will love you.

~ Vision ~

Start with one step

The journey of a thousand miles,
starts with one step.

~ Confucius ~

It is not impossible to avoid wrongdoing

Abandon wrong. It can be done.
If it were impossible to do
I would not urge you to do so.
But since it can be done
I say to you abandon wrong....

~ Buddha - A. ~

How to gain real happiness?

In cleansing the mind
And attaining wisdom,
One experiences joy, bliss, tranquillity,
Awareness, full understanding – real happiness.

~ Buddha - Ud ~

What is impossible?

Every noble work is at first impossible.

~ Thomas Carlyle ~

Misfortunes

Misfortunes always come in by the door
that has been kept open for them.

~ Czech proverb ~

When we make others happy, we too gain happiness

Happiness, the goal for which we all are striving, is reached by endeavouring to make the lives of others happy.

~ Mahatma Gandhi ~

All actions bear fruits

No matter what a man does, whether his deeds serve virtue or vice, nothing lacks importance. All actions bear a kind of fruit.

~ Buddha – Ud ~

You clean only outwardly

You ignorant!!
Of what use are your long locks?
Of what use your clothing of hides?
Within yourself darkness is at home.
Only outwardly you clean yourself.

~ Buddha – Ud ~

Respect

Respect is an important ingredient in life.
If we do not respect others
we may not treat them well.
Everyone deserves respect and
to be treated well.

~ Lessons in Enlightenment ~

8

Speech must be Guided

hat a unique faculty is the gift of speech! When we see the dumb, only then do we realise the human voice has the gift of expression. There is no musical instrument that could ever match the richness of the human voice. Through speech we have found the method of communication and developed human language.

One should be fearless but cautious in giving tongue to his thoughts; for a word uttered thoughtlessly and without due consideration may lead to chaos. In all our speech and writing we only make use of a few letters in the alphabet, but what marvels, wonders and utter destruction we can do with these few letters.

Words can bring us gain or loss, praise or blame, good repute or ill will, happiness or misery. A gentle word, at times, can melt the hardest heart. The Buddha tamed many vicious and unrefined men by kind and gentle words.

Unpleasant speech or a sarcastic smile may turn a good-natured man into a criminal, a friend into a foe. Much of the misunderstandings, dissension and animosities could be controlled, if not eliminated, if only people are more thoughtful and gentle in what they say, and more accurate and sincere in what they write. "Better than a thousand sentences — a mere jumble of meaningless words — is one sensible phrase on hearing which one is pacified," says the Buddha.

Even our dumb animals detest harsh language. We know how a dog manifests its appreciation by the wagging of its tail and the twisting of its body when it is spoken to in a gentle tone.

Know what not to say

Diplomacy is the art of knowing what not to say.

~ Matthew Trump ~

Qualities of a preacher

Whatever is in the sermon must be in the preacher first; clearness, logicalness, vivacity, earnestness must be personal qualities in him before they are qualities of the thought and language in what he utters.

~ Phillips Brooks ~

Speech and skill

A speech is like a love affair — any fool can start one, but to end takes considerable skill.

~ Lord Mancroft ~

Argument and agreement

There's too much said for the sake of argument and too little said for the sake of agreement.

~ Cullen Hightower ~

Speech must be Guided

Positive ideas help people to grow

Negative thoughts weaken men. Do you not find that where parents are constantly taxing their children to read and write, telling them they will never learn anything and calling them fools and so forth, the latter do actually turn out to be so in many cases?

If you speak kind words to children and encourage them, they are bound to improve in time. What holds good for children also holds well in the region of higher thoughts.

If you can give people positive ideas, they will mature and learn to stand on their own legs. In language and literature, in poetry and the arts in everything we must point out not the mistakes that people are making in their thoughts and actions, but the way in which they will gradually be able to do these things better. Pointing out mistakes wounds a man's feelings.

~ Swami Vivekananda ~

Why criticism is bad

Criticism with bad intention is futile because it puts a man on the defensive, and usually makes him strive to justify himself. It is dangerous, because it damages a man's precious pride, hurts his sense of importance, and arouses his resentment. Let's realise that the person we are going to correct and condemn will probably justify himself, and condemn us in return.

The talkative parrot

Much talking is a source of danger:
Through silence, misfortune is avoided
The talkative parrot in a cage is shut,
While birds that cannot talk fly freely.

~ Tibetan Yogi ~

Words can cut deeper than a sword

A blow with a word is deeper than a blow with a sword.

~ Robert Burton ~

Speech must be Guided

Flattery seldom strengthens our minds

We all like commendation and many of us like flattery, but it is a debatable question as to whether the indulgence of these tendencies builds character and strength and individuality.

~ Napoleon Hill ~

Silence

I believe in the discipline of silence and
can talk for hours about it.

~ George Bernard Shaw ~

We should not sacrifice truth for anything

Everything can be sacrificed for truth,
but truth cannot be sacrificed for anything.

~ Swami Vivekananda ~

We must know who we are

There is so much good in the worst of us and so much bad in the best of us, that it is hardly necessary for any of us to talk about the rest of us.

Do not talk ill of others

If you want people to think well of you,
do not speak ill of others.

Slander uncovers one's inner-self

The man who slanders his fellowmen unwittingly uncovers the real nature of his inner-self.

~ Napoleon Hill ~

Who talks much?

One who knows does not talk much.
One who does not know talks a lot.

~ Lao Tze ~

No one is free from blame

People blame others for their silence. They blame

those who talk much or in moderation.

There is therefore no one in this world who is not blamed.

There never was, nor will be, nor is there now, any one who is wholly blamed or wholly praised.

~ Buddha - Dh. ~

Think before you talk

Think well before you speak because your words may plant the seed of either success or failure in the mind of some other person.

~ Napoleon Hill ~

A wise man talks from his heart

The heart of a fool is in his mouth,
but the mouth of a wise man is in his heart.

~ Benjamin Franklin ~

Why people quarrel

When people cannot discuss
in a reasonable manner, usually they quarrel.

Speak less

We have two ears and only one tongue in order
that we may hear more and speak less.

~ Deogenes ~

Effective speech is acquired

The ability to speak effectively
is an acquirement rather than a gift.

~ William Jennings Bryan ~

Great ones observe silence

Brooks make so much noise
while the great river flows in silence.

~ Buddha - Sn. ~

Cracked vessel

A vessel is known by the sound, whether it is cracked or not, so men are proved by their speeches whether they be wise or foolish.

~ Demosthenes ~

Argument with a fool

When you are arguing with a fool,
you also become a fool.

The effect of harsh speech is never healed

Injury by an arrow will get healed. A tree cut by an axe will sprout again. But the wound inflicted by an unkind and harsh speech will never get healed.

~ Mahabharata ~

Two ways to indicate weakness

Two things indicate our weakness — to be silent when it is proper to speak, and to speak when it is proper to be silent.

Guard your tongue

If your foot slips you may recover your balance, but if your tongue slips you cannot recall your words.

~ Franklin ~

Difference between discussion and argument

Discussion is an exchange of intelligence; argument is an exchange of ignorance.

~ Washington Post ~

Good communication and coffee

Good communication is as stimulating as black coffee and just as hard to sleep after indulging in it.

~ Anne Morrow Lindburgh ~

Knowledge and wisdom

It is the province of knowledge to speak and it

is the privilege of wisdom to listen.

~ Oilver Wendell Holmes ~

Hands can speak

Other parts of the body assist the speaker but the hands speak themselves.

By them we ask, promise, invoke, dismiss, threaten, entreat, and disapprove.

By them we express fear, joy, grief, doubts, consent or repent; we show moderation or profusion, and mark number and time.

~ Quintilian ~

The fool should keep quiet

The fool can cover up his stupidity until he opens his mouth.

~ Sanskrit saying ~

Whether man is wise or a fool

For one word a man is often deemed to be

wise, and for one word he is often deemed to be foolish. We should be careful indeed what we say.

~ Confucius ~

Effective communication

When you speak so loudly,
I cannot hear what you say.

~ Ralph Waldo Emerson ~

Silent administrator

They that govern the most make the least noise.

~ John Seldon ~

Talk

Wise men talk because
they have something to say;
Fools because
they have to say something.

~ Plato ~

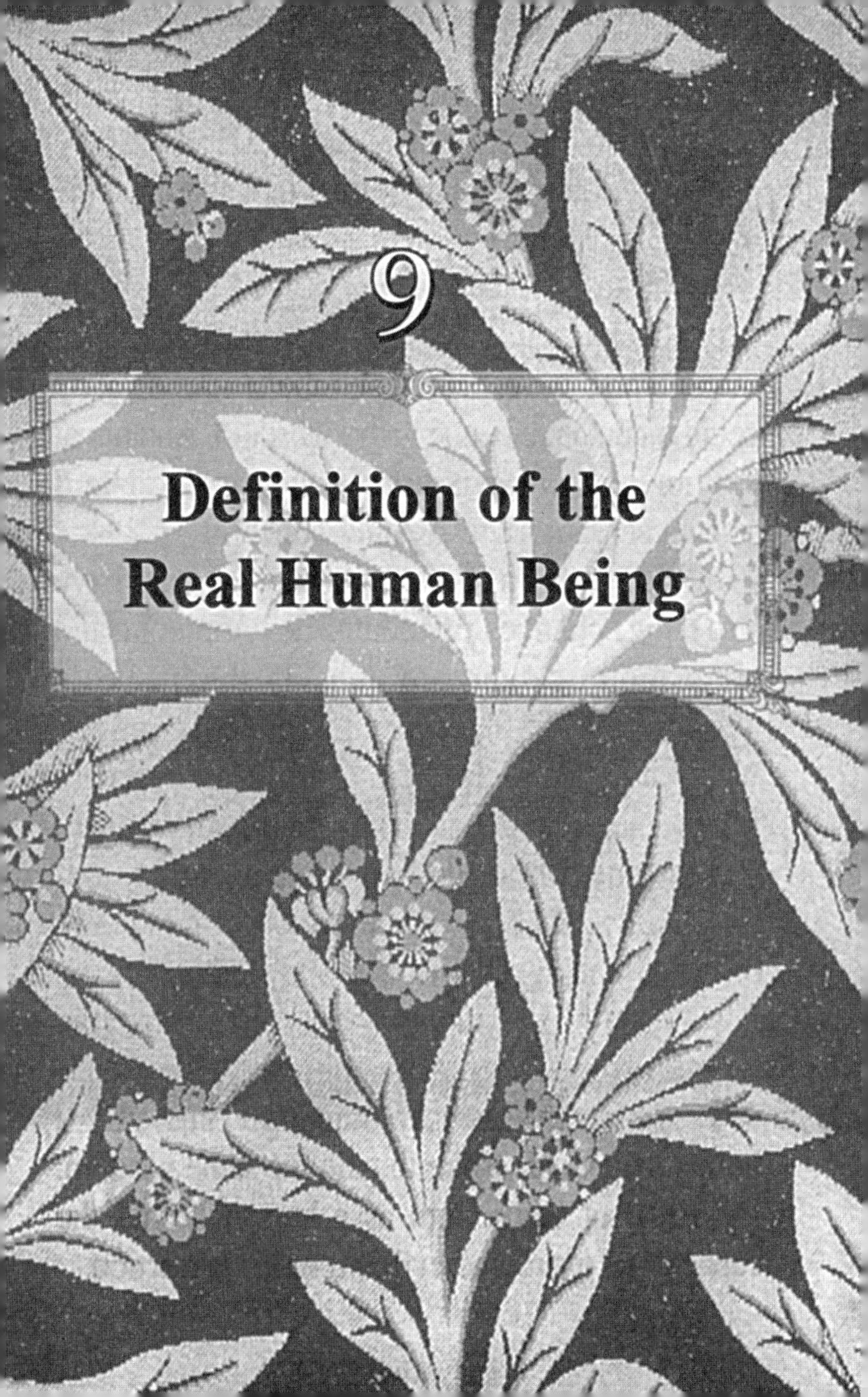

9

Definition of the Real Human Being

In the hierarchy of the inhabitants of the planetary system, of which the earth is a part, the position of the human being is relatively high, however insignificant he is in the universe in respect of numbers. It is only by being a human, can one gather wisdom. An animal cannot acquire wisdom, because food and self-preservation are its only concern.

If one is born in hell, undergoing intensive suffering, chances of mental development and cultivation of mind are poor. In the heavenly abodes, the deities have too much comfort, which does not help them to think and prepare for the next existence. They find it difficult to understand impermanency, uncertainty and unsatisfactoriness of life and do not make any effort to end repeated birth and death.

Only the human being is in a supreme position to elevate himself to higher planes of existence by superior thinking. Thus only a human being can aspire to gain the same wisdom. By virtue of being born as a human he has the capacity to overcome evil and reach perfection.

Definition of the Real Human Being

Earthly life as a human being is so important that all Buddhas attain their Enlightenment while being born human. It is needless to say that to kill a human being is a great offence, for he is the only being on earth who has the potential to cultivate kindness, compassion, honesty, goodwill and other humane qualities to serve the other living beings and to release them from their suffering, fear and worries.

By doing so, he develops his human values and prepares for his future existence and liberation. It is rare to be born as a human being.

The definition of man

- Chinese philosophy:
  man means 'human heartiness'.
- Greek philosophy:
  one who can use reasoning.
- Indian philosophy:
  one who has a perfected soul.
- Buddhism:
  one who excels all other beings in terms of mind and its development.

Who is a great man?

A great man shows his greatness
by the way that he treats
his poor fellow beings with compassion.

The worst enemy

Man is his own worst enemy.

~ Cicero ~

Definition of the Real Human Being

Who is regarded as a real man?

- A man without the feeling of mercy is not a man.
- A man without the feeling of deference and politeness is not a man.
- A man without feeling shame and dislike is not a man.
- A man without feeling right and wrong is not a man.

~ Mencius ~

We are responsible for our life

Human destiny can only be determined by human beings.

~ Albert Schweitzer ~

Man can become god

Buddhism upholds the view that man is an intelligent being. He surpasses even the devas (*gods*) in wisdom and strength.

The Bodhisatva left heaven and descended to this world in order to attain his enlightenment.

Gods do not have the ability to purify and develop their minds to attain enlightenment. Only man can gain such a status.

Where is the fate of a man?

The fate of a man is decided not by the whims of a supernatural being, but by his thoughts, words and deeds.

How to use income

Divide your income into four portions:

- One portion for your food.
- Two portions to fulfil duties and business needs
- Last portion to invest or deposit for the Future.

~ Buddha ~

Definition of the Real Human Being

Ten duties of human beings

- Ministering their parents
- Attending to their children
- Looking after their spouses
- Developing mutual understanding between husband and wife
- Attending to relatives
- Respecting the elders
- Remembering the departed ones by doing some religious services
- Inviting devas (divine beings) to share the happiness of merits that have been done
- Adjusting the way of life in accordance with a suitable environment
- Leading a righteous way of life.

~ Buddha - A. 10 ~

Faith in oneself is more important

Man may have faith in every god,
yet if he has no faith in himself, he is doomed.

~ Swami Vivekananda ~

Biologically humans are weak

Biologically, humans are weaker than many other beings, big or small. Other animals are born, armed with some sort of weapon for their own protection and survival. Humans on the other hand, have their mind for everything but they must not use it as a weapon.

Humans are regarded as cultured living beings because they are meant to harmonise with others and not to destroy them.

He who loves himself should not harm another

The whole wide world we traverse
with our thoughts,
And nothing finds a man more dear than self.
Since so dear the self to others is,
Let the man who loves himself
harm no other man.

~ Buddha - S. I: 75 ~

United Nations' Charter

It is not the Charter of the United Nations that has failed the international community; it is the international community that has failed to live up to its responsibilities under the Charter.

~ U Thant ~

The sweetest sound to man

Remember that a man's name is to him the sweetest and most important sound.

Human beings worry more

Human beings have more worries when they think of their lives, but other living beings are free in that respect.

Purity in human life

It is not through the partaking of meat that people become impure but through drunkenness, obstinacy, bigotry, deceit, envy, disparagement of others, and evil intention.

The Buddha and Jesus both have said that man's life is not made impure by the things that go into the body through the mouth, but the things that come out from their mouths.

Final corner

When you have turned all the corners and
run into yourself
Then you have turned all the corners that
are left.

~ C. Langston Hughes ~

The world within us

It is in this fathom-long body with its mind and perceptions that I declare lies the world, the origin of the world, the cessation of the world, and the way leading to the cessation of the world.

~ Buddha ~

How Buddha analyses human craving

Human beings are more selfish in their indulgence of sense pleasure than any other living beings. They enjoy worldly lives and sensual pleasures by disregarding the welfare of others or the survival of other species. They also like to live long to experience more pleasures.

It has been said that only man hoards more than he can eat. All other animals take only as much as they need for their survival. What they do not need, they leave for others.

Everything is there within man

Nothing happens to man that is not contained within man.

~ C. Jung ~

What lies within us

What lies behind us and what us lies before us are tiny matters compared to what lies within us.

~ Ralph Waldo Emerson ~

Man and universe

The universe can be found within man and is not to be derived from any reality outside man.

~ Mencius ~

The zoo is to study human habits

A zoo is a place devised for animals
to study the habits of human beings.

~ Oliver Herford ~

Heaven and hell on earth

In the teachings of the Buddha, it is mentioned that human beings experience heavenly bliss when the objects impinging on the five senses are favourable and soothing.

On the other hand, they also experience sufferings like in hell, if the objects are irritating and disturbing.

You should not become a burden to this world

You are born into this world to do some good and not to pass your time in idleness. If you are indolent, then you are a burden to this world. You must always think of rising higher in goodness and wisdom. You will be abusing the privileges of becoming a human being if you do not prove yourself worthy of the merit, which brought you here.

What you are is more important

Remember that your real wealth can be measured, not by what you have, but by what you are.

~ Napoleon Hill ~

Man leaves something behind after he is gone

All the progress in this world made by man is due to the fact that he realises he is mortal and that he would like to leave his mark behind after he is gone.

Judging a man

- See a good man,
  look well at him and try to emulate him;
- See a bad man,
  look well also, not at him but at yourself.

~ Confucius ~

Man's greed

The world has enough for everyone's needs, but never enough for even one man's greed.

~ Mahatma Gandhi ~

Ability to atone

The ability of a person to atone has always been the most remarkable of human features.

~ Leon Uris ~

No human values

High living and low thinking degrade human values.

Different ways of facing anger

There are three kinds of people in the world. The first are those who are like letters carved in rock; they easily give way to anger and retain their angry thoughts for a long time.

The second are those who are like letters written on sand; they give way to anger also, but their angry thoughts quickly fade away.

The third are those who are like letters written in running water; they do not retain their passing thoughts; they let abuse and uncomfortable gossip pass by unnoticed; their minds are always pure and undisturbed.

Man and animals

Wild animals never kill for sport. Man is the only one to whom the torture and death of his fellow creatures is amusing.

~ James Anthony Froude ~

Distinguishing humans and animals

The desire for food, sleep, fear and sex are common among all living beings, but human beings distinguish themselves in matters of Dharma.

If this Dharma is not in them, they are just like animals.

~ Hitopadesa ~

Life of a penniless man

- Better to live in the forest with fierce animals.
- Better to live on fruits properly ripened.
- Better to sleep on a mat made of grass.
- Better to use the bark as the dress than to live among relatives in poverty.

~ Hitopadesa ~

Human Frailty

I cannot imagine a god who rewards and punishes the objects of his creation, whose purposes are modelled after our own — a God, in short, who is but a reflection of human frailty.

~ Albert Einstein ~

A friend is needed

A friend in need is a friend indeed.
For what are friends?
As a staff to the lame.
As a tent in the rain.
A true friend is life's greatest gain.

~ Everyday Human Values ~

Two occasions when people cry

There are two kinds of people in the world:

- People who cry when you pass away.
- People who cry when you pass their way!

~ Sai Baba ~

Human life is a mixture

- The human being is a strange mixture of the instinctive animal, the emotional human and the inner-spiritual person.
- The groomed person is said to be one who has succeeded in 'taming the animal instincts' and human passions.
- The cultured person is said to be one who has triumphed over the 'selfish ego'.

Animal reacts and human responds

Somebody puts out some food for a dog. If you try to take the food away, he will 'woof' angrily. He goes for you without regard to who you are. He's just reacting. So animal nature is to react, that of humans is to respond.

~ Vision ~

Man is the architect of his fortune

Every man is the architect of his own fortune.

~ Sallust ~

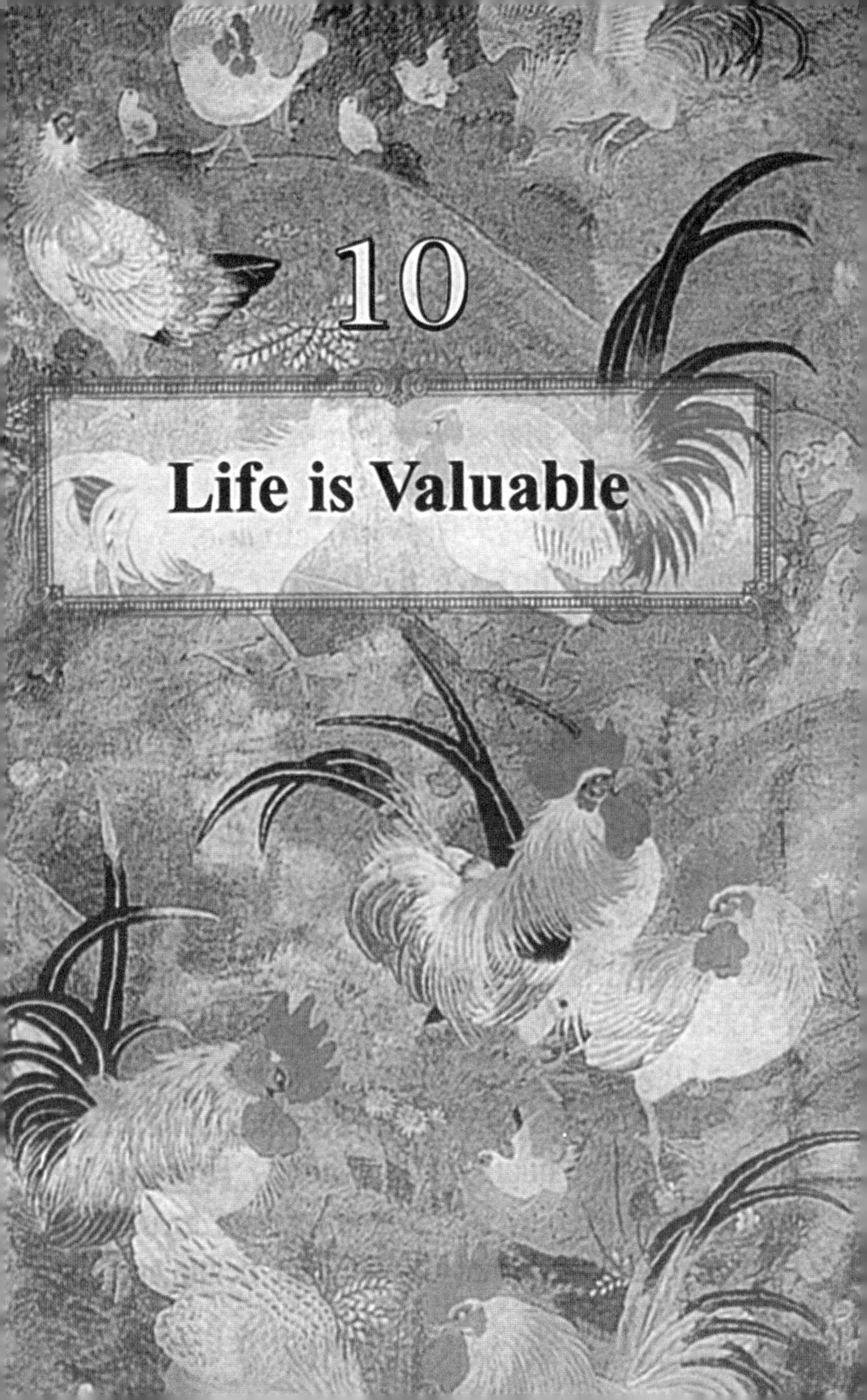

10

Life is Valuable

We live our lives in many foolish ways without even considering how much time we waste for anything. How much time have we wasted today worrying about next year, about the next twenty years, thinking about the future, to the extent that we have not been fully living even up to this very day!

Our values in life will change. What is important in life? What is motivating us? What is the driving factor in our lives? If we really contemplate death, it may cause us to reconsider our values. It does not matter how much property we have, for we cannot take any of it with us. Even our own body has to be left behind for others to dispose of in one way or another; it is just a heap of refuse left behind. We cannot take with us even any organ of our body, which we regard as very precious when we leave this world.

The quality of life is more important than mere material acquisitions. The quality of life is primarily the quality of our minds. How we are living today may be more important to us than many other external things. But death and the quality of the mind control the condition for rebirth. This is one thing we take with us. This is the one inheritance that we do not leave behind for others.

All that will follow us will be the qualities that we develop within us, the qualities of mind, the spiritual qualities and the good or bad qualities. These are all that we inherit. These are the conditions which will determine our rebirth and shape the future. These in turn will give rise to a new value in our lives. We may enjoy the millions we have already gained but it is more important that we live peacefully and start to build up some virtuous qualities. It can have a very good effect on the way we live our lives and on the values we develop. It is not just a matter of being successful; it is how we become successful.

What is life?

Life is nothing but a series of manifestations of becoming and extinction. It is a stream of becoming.

Life is blissful if we possess nothing

Blissful indeed is it to own nothing
When one is learned and
has mastered the Dharma.
See how people who own things are afflicted,
For people are strongly bound to people.

~ Buddha - Ud ~

Life is sacred

Life is sacred and must be properly guided. It must be cherished and fostered. Otherwise it can become a curse to the whole world. Peace is essential to life.

Love, compassion and care for all bring peace and make life worth living.

Four ways to realise the aim in life

- Material or physical wealth
- Likes and dislikes or pleasant and unpleasant feelings
- Studying and reasoning
- Sympathetic understanding; based on justice, purity and fair dealing.

The last one is the realistic and lasting method, which never creates disappointment.

How to cultivate divine life?

The Buddha says that man is capable of rising above all human weaknesses and cultivating a divine life through his own efforts.

Man is not for someone to experiment with

To the Buddha, man is not an experiment in life created by somebody to be done away with as sinners, when unwanted.

Life is changeable

Not knowing the real nature of life, we try to live without experiencing any disappointments and changes.

But life is changeable. It is a bundle of elements and energies, which are always changing and will not always be to our satisfaction.

What is the age limit to be old?

The Buddha was once asked at
what age a person become old.
The Buddha's reply was:
Any time the person
perceptibly feels he or she is old.

The purpose of life

Is there a purpose for life?
What is the purpose of life?
What, or where, or when?
Out of space came universe,
Came sun, came earth, came life,

Life is Valuable

Came man, and more must come,
But as to purpose:
Whose or whence?
Why, None!

Face facts in life

Life is as fleeting as a rainbow,
A flash of lightning,
a star at dawn.
Knowing this, how can you quarrel?

~ Jack Kornfield ~

What to do with life

In fact, life is a unique experience. There is nothing with which to compare it; no measure of its value could be determined in terms of some other things, and money cannot purchase it.

Yet, many have not learned what to do with this 'priceless jewel'. Here, life does not mean mere physical body or senses, but the thinking human mind.

It is difficult to have a smiling face when life goes wrong

It is easy enough to be pleasant
When life flows along like a song
But the man worthwhile
Is the man who can smile
When life goes dead wrong.

The world is not big enough to record human miseries

If all the mountains were books and if all the lakes were ink and if all the trees were pens, still they would not suffice to depict all the misery in this world.

~ Jacob Boehme ~

Harmonise with other living beings

Life is dear to every living being.
It is unfair to deprive them of their right to live.

Nature of our life

We live and work and dream,
Each has his little scheme,
Sometimes we laugh;
Sometimes we cry
And thus the days go by.

Do not become a slave to desire

He, who is discontented, however much he possesses, becomes a slave to his desires. All the sages have declared from the housetops that man can be his own worst enemy as well as his best friend. To be free or to be a slave lies in his own hand.

~ Mahatma Gandhi ~

How can there be a life without separation?

The Buddha reminded us that everything that exists is impermanent. With birth there is death;

with arising, there is dissolving; with coming together, there is separation.

How can there be birth without death? How can there be arising without dissolving? How can there be coming together without separation?

Life is short

Brief is the life of men
The wise man should not take delight therein.
Let him act as if his head was burning on fire.
For there is no way whereby death comes not.

~ Buddha - S. I: 108 ~

Fleeting nature of life

Life, personality, pleasure and pain
These last but one thought moment
Thus, suddenly everything passes away.

~ Buddha - Vism: 48 ~

Life is Valuable

Paying the price

Life wastes itself while we are preparing to live. Sickness, old age, and miseries are the payment we are making for occupying this body of ours as a house. We have to pay the price of fear and worry for creating selfish desires through our body.

Life must reach its destiny

Once life is launched, like a bullet it rushes to its destination — death.

The three fires that destroy everything

The fire of lust burns mortals
Infatuated by sensual pleasure;
The fire of hate burns malevolent people
Who kill other living beings.

The fire of delusion burns the bewildered,
Ignorant of the Noble One's Dharma.
Being unaware of these three fires,
Humankind delights in personal existence.

~ Buddha - It ~

Life exists after death

The body may die but there is life after death.

Even the philosopher Plato, who lived over two thousand years ago and had no idea of revealed religion, held this belief.

Unable to see the meaning of life

It is hardly surprising that today, in this so called highly advanced society, dominated by greed, fear and hatred, an increasing number of people should feel insecure and frustrated, and unable to see any meaning in life.

Things exist because of changes

No matter how strong a life is,
it is not secure,
not free from suffering, conflicts,
unsatisfactoriness and changes.

Impermanence and changes are the core of existing things.

Existence

We do not exist but struggle for existence.

Greek concept of the soul

There are three forms of soul:

- Vegetative soul provides
  the function of nutrition.
- Animal soul provides
  the sense of organs and organs of movements.
- The rational part is non-mortal and
  survives after death.

~ Aristotle ~

This is not the first and last life

According to Buddhism, our existence does not begin with this human life nor does it end with this life in eternal heaven or hell afterward. We have been existing in countless shapes and sizes according to our accumulated karma and will.

We continue to exist until the whole process

is understood and gradually brought to a standstill by our own strenuous and individual effort.

Without physical body there is no suffering

Suffering comes from having a body. Without a body how could there be suffering or misfortune?

~ Lao Tze ~

Whether there is life hereafter or not

Not knowing even what this life is, why do we care whether there will be another life?

~ Confucius ~

Thirst for survival

The birth of man is the birth of sorrow. The longer he lives the more stupid he becomes. What bitterness! He lives for what is always out of reach! His thirst for survival in the future makes him incapable of living in the present.

~ Chuang Tzu ~

Craving for needs

No one can live without craving. Craving is indispensable for living. The more you live the more you struggle for your survival and pleasures.

In this battle, you commit many mistakes by violating the peace and happiness of others. The method that you adopt for living creates many other problems, which you complain about almost everyday.

Only after maturity, understanding appears

When I was 18, I thought what a fool my father was. Now that I am 28, I am surprised how much the old man has learned in 10 years!

Actually, it is not the father who has learned, but the youth that has learned to see things in a mature way.

Life departs peacefully when there is no attachment

Whatever beings are born or will be born,
They will journey on, leaving the body.

Knowing that all must be abandoned,
A skilful one, ardent, should lead the holy life.

~ Buddha - Ud ~

Five things difficult to gain

Long life, beauty, happiness, honour and heavenly bliss.

~ Buddha ~

Life must have an aim

An aimless life is always a miserable life.

Good life is more important than long life

A long life may not be good enough,
but a good life is long enough.

~ Benjamin Franklin ~

Middle Path - moderate way of life

All religions follow a course of training in order to groom the 'inner-self'.

Life is Valuable

The avoidance of extremes of self-indulgence and self-mortification are characteristic of Buddhist training. The Middle Way is the avoidance of both extremes, eternalism and annihilation.

The Buddha advised people to follow this Middle Path in every aspect of their lives. But many people have not realised the real meaning and usefulness of this noble Middle Path. The deeper meaning of this Middle Path goes beyond the concern with righteous behaviour, avoiding extremes and taking a moderate course in life. The deeper meaning is learning how to use our human sense faculties most effectively, without misuse or abuse.

Our own defilements destroy life

Greed, hatred and delusion,
Arisen from within himself,
Harm an evil-minded person
As its own fruit (*flower*)
destroys the bamboo tree.

~ Buddha - It ~

The six basic fears which diminish self-confidence

- The fear of poverty,
- The fear of old age,
- The fear of criticism,
- The fear of loss of love of someone,
- The fear of ill health,
- The fear of death.

~ Napoleon Hill ~

Struggling for living

In the eyes of the Buddha, living beings tremble like fish in a stream that is almost dry, being in the grip of craving, either leaping hither and thither, like hares caught in a snare or lost like arrows shot at night.

He saw the struggle of all against all, the senseless series of predators trying to prey upon or rob their victims.

Everything is uncertain

- World is uncertain,
- Philosophy is theoretical,
- Politics is hypocritical,
- Religion has become irrational,
- Science is inhuman,
- Psychology is imaginative,
- Education is job orientated,
- Man is unreliable,
- Mind is changeable.

Fear can ruin our life

- Fear fills a person with perpetual mental tension and anguish.
- Fear progressively erodes life and debases the mind.
- Fear is a potent pessimistic force, which darkens the future.
- If one harbours any kind of fear,
- his way of thinking will be affected.
- Fear is capable of eroding one's personality and making him landlord to a ghost.

What is a useful life?

- What is wealth,
  which is neither distributed nor enjoyed?
- What is power,
  which is not exercised to stop enemies?
- What is knowledge,
  which is not coupled with Dharma?
- What is life,
  which is not being disciplined?

~ Hitopadesa ~

We like to have a permanent life

Our mind needs a permanent life but life creates an impermanent physical body and we take this as life. In fact what we need for our satisfaction is not an immortal life but freedom from the concept of immortality. Life is in a state of flux and it is never static.

Every moment we are marching towards the graveyard. Birth and death are two ends of the same string; we cannot do away with death and choose to have existence only.

Life is Valuable

Man fools himself

Man fools himself.
He prays for a long life, but he fears old age.

~ Chinese proverb ~

Unsatisfactoriness is the nature of life

- Unsatisfactoriness follows one
  like a shadow along the pathway of life.
- During childhood,
  he has to shoulder the demands of duty.
- In the prime of manhood,
  he struggles to support himself and his family.
- The declining years bring sickness,
  weakness, dependency, loneliness,
  suffering and finally death.
- Such is the fate of humanity.

One who never fails

The one who never fails,
is the one who never tried.

Impermanency in life

My life is like the summer rose
That opens to the morning sky,
But as the shades of evening close
Is scattered on the ground — to die.

~ Wilde ~

Fight within yourself

When a man's fight begins within himself,
he is worth something.

~ Robert Browning ~

What will happen when we grow old?

As we grow old, we become both
more foolish and wiser.

~ Rochefoucauld ~

Not to grow old

That man never grows old
who keeps a child in his heart.

Happy old fellow

A healthy old fellow,
who is not a fool,
is the happiest creature living.

~ Steele ~

Who never grows old?

Some men never seem to grow old. Always active in thought, always ready to adopt new ideals, they are never changeable with egoism.

Satisfied, yet ever dissatisfied, settled, yet ever unsettled, they always enjoy the best of what is, and are the first to find the best of what will be. Though I look old, yet I am strong and lusty.

~ Shakespeare ~

Working without living!

We have too many people who live without working, and we have altogether too many who work without living.

~ Dean Chartes R. Brown ~

Cultivate the heart

The heart is like a garden.
It can grow compassion or fear,
Resentment or love.
What seeds will you plant there?

~ Jack Kornfield ~

The cosmic laws

Always bear in mind the Three Cosmic Laws
Or universal principles of impermanence,
Suffering and non-self or emptiness
That governs all mundane existence.
These are important keys
to understanding you and life,
And keys to open the doors
of universal truth and reality.

~ Lessons in Enlightenment ~

11

Nature is the Creator

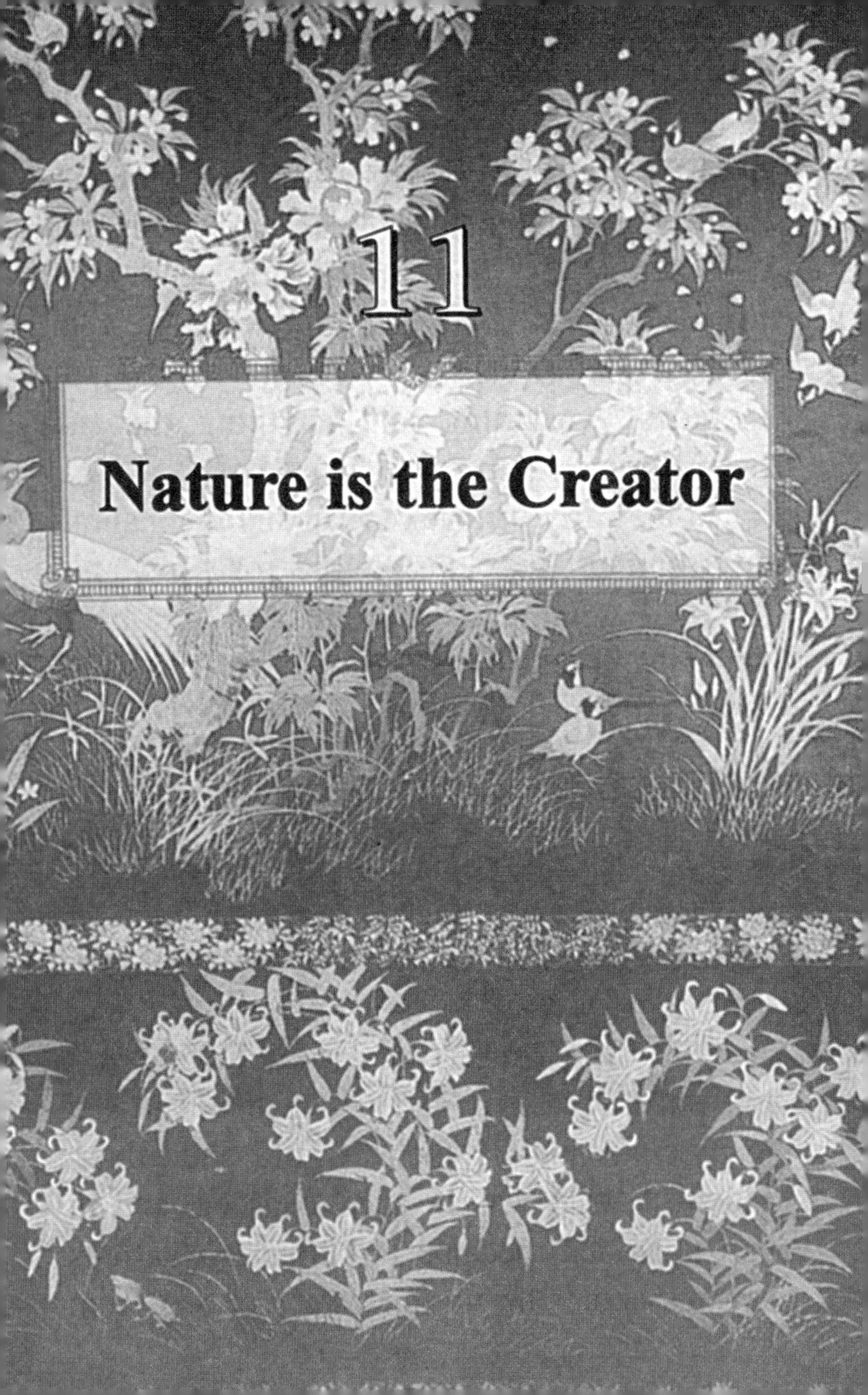

ature involves our natural surroundings. It includes trees, birds, bacteria, clouds, wind, rocks, stars, etc. It also includes sounds we can hear, heat that we can feel, gravity that pulls us to the earth. In short, it includes everything and anything that is 'natural', that is, not made by anybody.

In the early history of mankind the natural environment was the source for food and shelter. Natural materials were used to fashion tools and natural fires were tamed to provide heat and light. The calls of animals could indicate danger or mere contentment and man learned to know the difference because life depended on a large part upon such knowledge.

Lightning and thunder were frightening until their nature was understood. Man was curious about his surroundings and tried to find out just how ordinary rocks or minerals might be changed to precious metals such as gold and silver. Much of what was in part observed, and in part-imagined, became folklore, and various sayings about the weather were passed from generation to generation. When a written language was developed much of what had been passed by word of mouth became a written record and many aspects of nature were included in such writings. The great religious leaders found that the use of common place knowledge about nature could be made the basis of their moral and ethical lessons.

More and more people are growing aware of our dwindling natural resources. Thus, there is added impetus to the hope that an understanding and love of nature will bring about a public opinion that will safeguard and conserve our resources, so that our future generations can have much to study and enjoy in our natural environment.

Buddhism has always been associated with nature. The Buddha was born under a tree and gained enlightenment under a tree and spent many hours in the seclusion of jungles. He even passed away under the shade of two trees.

He always extolled the great benefit to be derived from association with nature. He discouraged the destruction of plants and animals for the pleasure.

What is nature?

Nature is made up of conflicting processes and forces. Socrates said that nature is not an accidental chaos as the previous sophists had thought but is rather an ordered array of interacting agencies, which on the whole support one another. Thus each part of the human organism serves the other and benefits the whole.

Panca Niyama Dharma – Fivefold Law or natural order of existence

- *Utu Niyama*: refers to the physical, inorganic order. This order includes such phenomena as the seasonal winds and rains, the unerring sequence of the four seasons, characteristic seasonal changes and events, the causes of wind and rains, the nature of heat, etc.
- *Bija Niyama*: refers to the physical organic order. This order includes such phenomena as germs and seeds: How rice is produced from rice seed, how sugar taste results from sugar cane or honey, the peculiar characteristics of certain fruits, etc. The scientific theory of cells and genes

and the physical similarity of twins may be ascribed to this order.

- *Karma Niyama*: refers to the order of action (condition) and result. This natural law states that desirable and undesirable acts produce corresponding good and bad results. As surely as water seeks its own level, so does karma, given opportunity, produce its inevitable result — not in the form of reward or punishment but as an innate sequence. This sequence of cause and effect is as natural and necessary as the way of the sun and the moon.
- *Dharma Niyama*: refers to the order of the norm; e.g. the natural phenomena occurring at the advent of a Bodhisatva in his last birth, gravitation and other similar laws of nature. Morality and so forth may be included in this group.
- *Citta Niyama*: refers to the order of the mind or psychic laws. This order includes such phenomena as processes of consciousness, constituents of consciousness, power of mind, etc. All psychic phenomena, which are

inexplicable to modern science, are included in this order: telepathy, telesthesia, retrocognition, premonition, clairvoyance, clairaudience, thought reading, etc.

~ Buddhist View ~

How Buddhism supports the environment

One who has taken shelter under a tree should not cut down even its branches. He who does that is an ungrateful person.

Those who plant trees, which give shelter and fruits to living beings, earn merits.

~ Jataka Tale ~

Impermanency in everything

Nations grow and die out; empires arise and fall apart; mighty palaces are built and crumble in the dust — such is the way of the world.

Beautiful flowers blossom and attract all that pass by; but the next day they fade and dry up. Their petals all drop one by one and soon they are forgotten altogether. Forests may be turned into cities and cities into sand dunes. Where mountains exist, a lake may be formed.

All enjoyments and high attainments of the world are only a momentary show. One who takes pleasure in them has to lament and weep when they are lost, and undergoes much suffering due to lack of understanding of impermanence.

The law of impermanence

Look at the people in the world,
Afflicted by ignorance,
Come into being,
Delighting in being, not freed.
Whatever forms of being exist,
In any way, anywhere,
All these forms of being are impermanent,
Subject to suffering, of a nature to change.

~ Buddha - Ud ~

Law without freedom

Constitutional reform without free citizenship is like rich attire on a dead body. Better to breathe good free air than be a corpse in the finest raiment.

Do not go against nature

Those who lead their lives by violating natural ways of life and environment must face the consequences either physically or mentally.

Faith and bird

Faith is a bird that can see the light
when it is dawn and starts singing in the dark.

~ Dr. Rabindranath Tagore ~

Contemplation for reducing fear, worries and tension

- I am of the nature to age;
- I have not gone beyond ageing;
- I am of the nature to sickness;
- I have not gone beyond sickness;
- I am subjected to my own karma and
- I am not free from karmic effects;

Nature is the Creator

- I am of the nature to die,
- I have not gone beyond dying; and

All that is mine, beloved and pleasing, will change, will become otherwise, and will become separated from me.

~ Buddha ~

Seeking something in a darkroom which is not there

There is nowhere to hide from the truth of impermanence. Seeking an eternal soul is like searching a thing in a dark room, which is not there.

The world is in the dark

The world is held in bondage by delusion
And only appears to be capable.
To a fool, held in bondage by clinging
And wrapped up in darkness,
It appears to be eternal,
But for one who sees, there is nothing.

~ Buddha - Ud ~

Nature still forgives man

In the name of progress, the world has been wrecked by human beings for their personal comfort, disregarding the environment and all living things. Up until now, nature has been most forgiving. Man has to realise that this planet was not made for him to rape and plunder at will, and deprive other living things of their natural rights, but to live in accordance with nature.

Man is not a cosmic accident

Man is not a cosmic accident, but a culminating phase of the whole natural order with a peculiar and important function to perform. He alone can bring nature into the light of understanding and consciously direct his life and activities into voluntary harmony with this order.

~ Socrates ~

Morality is the law of nature

Morality is the backbone of religion and humanity. To lead a moral life is to lead a natural life because morality is the law of nature.

Struggling for existence

Every living thing including plants is struggling to exist. Yet this struggle always fails because the law of impermanence operates.

The world is not for human beings alone

The world was not made for human beings alone, nor is the world always made out in their favour.

Worldly conditions have no favouritism; they are neither kind nor cruel but neutral. Human beings exist because nature allows them to do so. It is the duty of human beings to understand the real worldly condition.

We must adapt ourselves to the environment

We have modified our environment so radically that we must modify ourselves to exist in this new environment.

~ N. Wiemer ~

There is nothing perfectly good or bad

The world situation is not always in our favour. There could be no world and life without problems. Even sunlight, rain, wind and moonlight welcomed by many, could be a nuisance to others. There is in fact nothing perfectly bad or perfectly good in this world.

World is nothing but waves

We are part of the same waves.
A man must be aware
Of the states of his body,
Of his feelings,
Of the states of his mind and
Of the states of mental objects.
All matter is made of waves and
we live in a world of waves.

~ Albert Einstein ~

Do not follow traditions blindly

We are living in an ever-changing world. We should not cling blindly to the traditions, customs and manners, rites and rituals practised by our forefathers or ancestors, who adopted these practices according to the beliefs and conditions prevalent during their time.

Poor countries will be trapped

Poor countries that approach the big nations with begging bowls for alms and economic aid fall into a trap and lose their independence.

Peace-loving people are crying and begging big nations to stop their nuclear arms race. But they turn deaf ears to this human cry and carry on developing more armaments capable of annihilating the whole of mankind. Small nations are used as scapegoats for their ulterior motives.

Can the universe revolve around us?

Can you imagine if Galileo had been a baby boomer? He would have proved that the universe revolved around him.

~ Jay Trachman ~

How to measure your age

There are three kinds of ages.
Chronological age is marked by the calendar.
Mental age is the compiling of wisdom.
Emotional age is how old you feel.

Continuity of life

Look at the sea; wave follows wave, it is not the same wave, yet one causes another and transmits its form and movement.

So the beings travelling through the world are not the same today and tomorrow, nor in one life the same as in another, and yet it is the urge and the form of the previous lives that determine the character of those that follow. A reasonable belief but incredible.

~ Somerset Maugham ~

Obstacles give opportunity

Without obstacles there would be no opportunities.

The animal that laughs and weeps

Man is the only animal that laughs and weeps for he is the only animal who knows the difference between what things are and what they ought to be.

~ William Hazlitt ~

Decision and action

Decision is the spark that ignites action.
Until a decision is made, nothing happens.

~ Wilfred Peterson ~

The way to reduce hostility

If we could read the secret history of our enemies, we would find in each man's life, sorrow and suffering enough to disarm all hostility.

~ Henry Wadsworth Longfellow ~

Jokes and nuts

Jokes are like nuts —
the drier they are the easier they crack.

Act accordingly

Like a beautiful flower full of colour but without scent are the empty words of him who does not act accordingly.

~ Buddha ~

Who is blind, dumb, poor and rich?

- The man who cannot see
  the difference between right and wrong is blind.
- The man who cannot say
  a kind word at the right time is dumb.
- The man plagued with
  too strong desires is poor.
- The man whose heart is contented is rich.

~ Indian philosophy ~

The way that we treat animals measure our greatness

The greatness of a nation and
its moral progress can be
judged by the way its animals are treated.

~ Mahatma Gandhi ~

What is enough?

You never know what is enough,
unless you know
what is more than enough.

How long we have existed

The bones of a single person
Accumulated in a single aeon
Would make a heap like a mountain —
So said the Great Sage.

~ Buddha - It ~

The camel and the diplomat

Q. *What is the difference between a camel and a diplomat?*

A. A camel can work for days without drinking, whereas a diplomat can drink for days without working.

Who makes history?

History, although sometimes made up of the few acts of the great, is more often shaped by the many acts of the small.

~ Mark Yost ~

What is future?

I never think of the future.
It comes soon enough.

~ Albert Einstein ~

The uneducated is not acknowledged

One, who is uneducated though gifted with good complexion, youth and born in high-class family, is not being acknowledged just as flower without fragrance.

~ Hitopadesa ~

You are the world

The world is made up of people; people make up the world. If you change the people, you are changing the world.

And you start with yourself. After all, are you also not one of the people in the world?

~ Bhikkhu Visuddhacara ~

Sympathise with inferiors

We should be patient with our inferiors,
they are ourselves of yesterday.

Without hope, no despair

He who has never hoped can never despair.

~ George Bernard Shaw ~

Good times fly, hard times linger

- When you are courting a nice girl, an hour seems like a second.
- When you sit on a red-hot cinder, a second seems like an hour. That's relativity.

~ Albert Einstein ~

Whose picture do you see first?

When you see a group photograph
that you are in,
whose picture do you look at first?

Some are happy hating others

Few people can be happy unless they hate some other person.

~ Bertrand Russell ~

Real vision

Vision without action is a dream.
Action without vision passes time.
Vision and action can change the world.

~ Vision ~

Vision of star

On a cloudy day, the star cannot be seen. Is the star there? Yes! When the bright sun shines, the star cannot be seen. Is the star there? Yes!

~ Vision ~

Nothing for us to claim as ours

We do not possess our home, our children, or even our own body. They are only given to us for a short while to treat with care and respect.

~ Jack Kornfield ~

Eight edges of the world

The world has eight edges, and each edge is razor sharp, capable of slicing human beings to bits without mercy. The eight edges of the world are, on the one side, the edge of wealth, the edge of status, the edge of praise and the edge of pleasure. These four edges are especially sharp because they're things we like. We keep polishing and sharpening them, and the more we do this the sharper they get, until ultimately they turn around and slit our throats.

The other side has four edges too, but actually they're not so sharp, because no one likes to use them. No one wants them, so no one sharpens them, and as a result they're dull and blunt — and like dull knives, they can't kill anyone. These four edges are loss of wealth, loss of status, criticism and pain. No one wants any of these things, but they have to exist as part of the world.

More troubles come from our own kind

A dog took a trip to see the country. A few days later he returned, and his friends asked him whether he faced problems on the trip.

He said that he had met many people and animals along the way. They did not create any disturbances but allowed him to go his way.

"The only problem I faced was from our own kind," he said. "They did not leave me alone. They barked at me and chased and tried to bite me."

Ending aggravates the situation

A dying candle flickers the brightest light.

Nature is the Creator

Three monkeys on a tree

Three monkeys sat on a coconut tree
Discussing things as they are said to be,
Said one to the others,

"Now listen, you two,
There is a certain rumour that just can't be true:
That man descended from our noble race.
The very idea of it is just a disgrace!

No monkey ever deserted his wife,
Starved her babies or ruined her life;
And another thing you will never see:
A monkey fences off a coconut tree,
And let the coconuts go to waste,
Forbidding other monkeys to come and taste.

If I put a fence around this tree,
Hunger would force you to steal from me,
And there is something else a monkey won't do:
Go out at night and get in a stew,
And use a gun or club or knife,
To take some other poor monkey's life."

One and only you

Every single blade of grass,
And every flake of snow —
Is just a wee bit different.
There's no two alike, you know.

From something small, like grains of sand,
To each gigantic star
All were made with this in mind:
To be just what they are!

How foolish then, to imitate —
How useless to pretend!
Since each of us comes from a mind
Whose ideas never end?

There'll only be just one of me
To show what I can do —
And you should likewise feel very proud,
There's only one of you.

That is where it all starts
With you, a wonderful unlimited human being.

~ James T. Moore ~

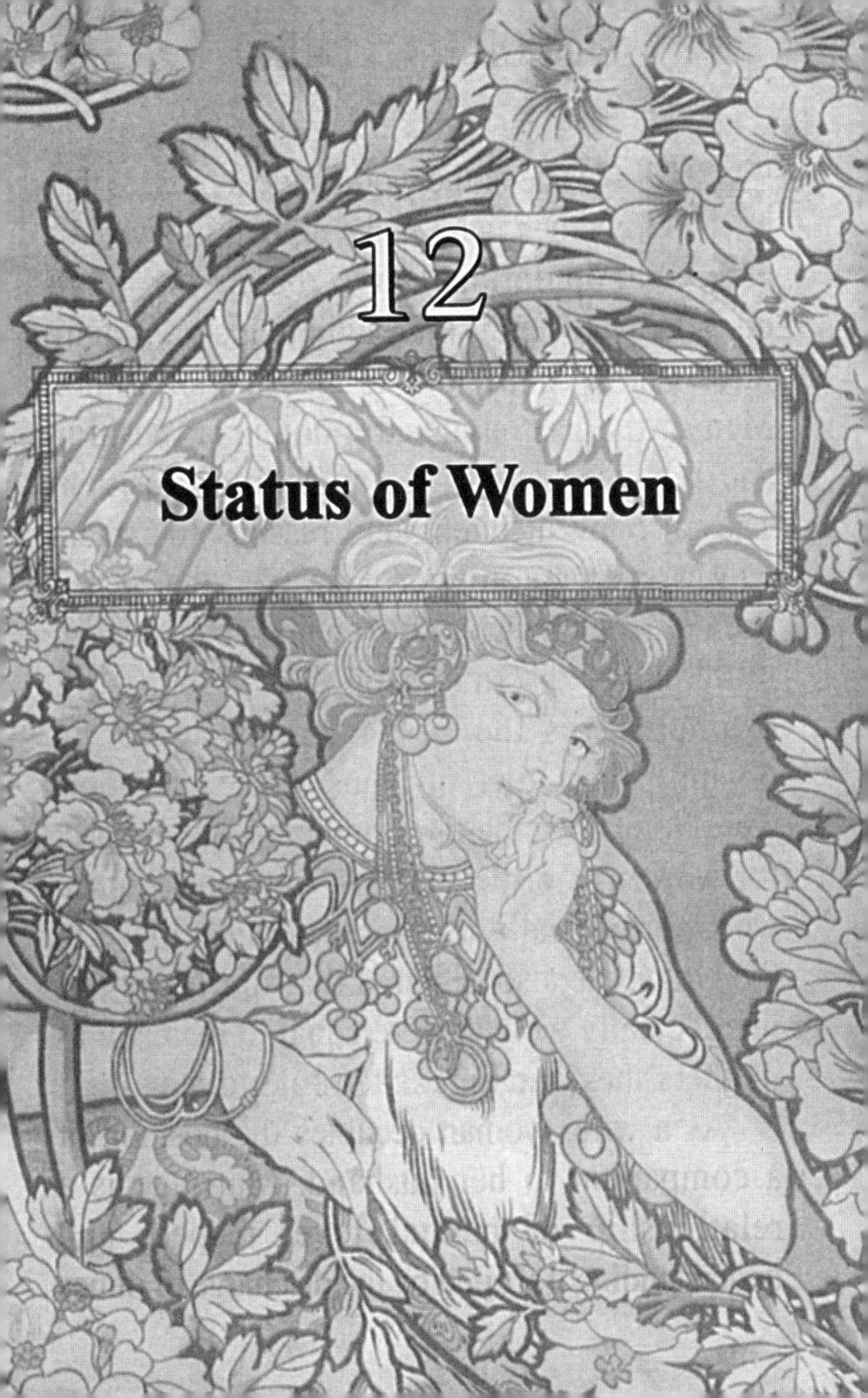

12

Status of Women

It is one of the world's great puzzles that women, who make up half the world's population, have been so much discriminated against throughout history. Many factors have contributed to this state of affairs. Men in the past assumed a dominant position and relegated women to an inferior position. They also invented religious 'reasons' to explain why women are inferior. However, there have been others who have spoken and acted against this kind of discrimination. The Buddha, for example, was the first religious leader to organise the Order of Nuns. Once the doors were flung open there was an immediate impact for women of all levels of society and women who were socially ostracised, found solace in the Order. He also declared that spiritually and intellectually women were equal to men and as mothers they had an exalted role to play.

As a wife, woman occupies the position of a companion to her husband. Marriage is a relationship of mutual love, respect and understanding, fortified by the discharge of duties towards one another. The *Sigalovada Sutta* clearly defines the duties of husband and wife. The wife in such a set-up, has a full active role to play exercising her authority and discretion with prudence and responsibility. She is not only accepted and respected as a person; she is even depended upon as a helpmate who has a unique positive contribution to make. As a mother, the woman was definitely honoured and revered and her position in society was unassailable.

In the next millennium, women will play an increasingly important role in the development of society. It is necessary for us to prepare them for that role by giving them equal opportunities to participate in every field of human endeavour. At the same time, however, women must not see the bringing up of a family as degrading. The traditional role of a mother as a caregiver must never be abandoned. What we need to do today, is to establish a balance between the two sexes, and refrain from the tendency to see them in confrontation with each other.

The hand that rules the world

The hand that rocks the cradle
Is the hand that rules the world

~ W. R. Wallace ~

Man's will and woman's way

Man has his will, but woman has her way.

A home in a house

A home is something that cannot be bought. You can buy a house but only a woman can make of it a home.

~ Napoleon Hill ~

Where is paradise?

When Prophet Mohammed was asked where paradise is, he said that paradise is at the feet of the mother.

A virtuous woman

Such a virtuous lady
who possesses religious devotion,
Cultivates virtue, is endowed with
Wisdom and learning
Makes a success of her life in this very existence.

~ Buddha - S. IV: 250 ~

She is indispensable

She is indispensable, because through her, Bodhisatvas and world rulers take birth.

~ Commentary ~

Five powers that make a woman confident

- The power of beauty,
- The power of wealth,
- The power of kinship,
- The power of procreation,
- The power of virtue.

But it is due to the power of virtue that a woman is reborn in fortunate states after death.

~ Buddha - S. IV: 239-250 ~

Woman has an important role to play in society

The hostile attitude to women both in religion and in society was repeatedly criticised and challenged by the Buddha on numerous occasions. In the Kosala Samyutta, the Buddha challenged the belief that the birth of a daughter was not as much a cause for joy as that of a son. The Buddha pointed out clearly that woman has a dignified and an important part to play in society, and he defined it with great insight, fitting her harmoniously into the social fabric. She is a loveable member of the household, held in place by numerous relationships, and respected above all, as the mother of worthy children. Gender did not matter, he argued, and added that in character and in her role in society, she could even rival men.

Difficulty of knowing the age of a woman

A woman vegetable seller was caught by the police for selling illicit liquor when she was taken to the court.

The judge asked, “How old are you?”
She replied, “I am 35 years old.”

The judge on checking her past records noted that she had declared her age as 35, five years ago for another offence.
Puzzled, the judge asked, “How can you be 35 today?”
She then said, “My Lord I am a woman of principle. I have no two words. I never change what I have said earlier especially in the court.”

Imagination of a lady

A lady’s imagination is very rapid; it jumps from admiration to love, from love to matrimony in a moment.

~ Jane Austen ~

Spiritual strength of woman

The strong disbelief held by men in women’s spiritual attainments, even after the recognised success of the nuns’ order, is beautifully illustrated by the statement made by the Buddha to Gotami when she visited him on the eve of her death.

"O Gotami, perform a miracle in order to dispel the wrong views of those foolish men who are in doubt with regards to the spiritual potentialities of women."

Women are not inferior

Mara: "No woman with her two finger-wisdom, could ever hope to reach the heights which are attained only by the sages."

Arahant Bhikkuni Soma: "When one's mind is well concentrated and wisdom never fails, does the fact of being a woman make any difference?"

Women are also wise

The belief that woman was intellectually
inferior to man was refuted in Buddhism.
Some women are better than men.
There are women who are wise and virtuous.

~ Buddha ~

Heart argues with woman

With woman, the heart argues not the mind.

~ Matthew Arnold ~

Women should not mimic men

I do believe that woman will not make her contribution to the world by mimicking or running a race with man.

She can run the race, but she will not rise to the great heights she is capable of by mimicking man. She should recognise and develop her own unique qualities.

~ Mahatma Gandhi ~

Self-sacrifice is more important

There must be no thought of man or woman being superior.

Each is complementary to the other, a partnership of equality, exuding gentleness, generosity, calm and dedication and most important of all, self-sacrifice.

Where heaven and hell are

Heaven has no rage like love to hatred turned,
Nor hell a fury like a woman scorned.

~ William Congreve ~

Difficulty of handling a fool

The silliest woman can manage a clever man, but it needs a very clever woman to manage a fool.

~ Rudyard Kipling ~

Where beauty lies

Beauty lies in the eyes of the beholder.

Mothers are philosophers

Mothers are the most instinctive philosophers.

~ Harriet Beecher Stowe ~

Indispensable to each other

As unto the bow the cord is,
So unto the man is woman;
Though she bends him,
she obeys him,
Though she draws him,
yet she follows;
Useless each without the other.

~ Henry Wadsworth Longfellow ~

Woman's intuition is grave

A woman's intuition has often proved truer than man's arrogant assumption of knowledge.

~ Mahatma Gandhi ~

How woman can change the man

A mother takes twenty years to make a man of her boy and another woman makes a fool of him in twenty minutes.

~ Robert Frost ~

Why women are in front

I asked a man why women, after centuries of following their men, now walk in front. He said there were many unexploded land mines since the war.

~ Robert Mueller ~

Two faults in men and many in women

Women have many faults; men have only two — everything they say and everything they do.

Who is the best husband?

An archaeologist is the best husband any woman can have, the older she gets, the more interest he has in her.

~ Agatha Christie ~

What is money for?

If women didn't exist, all the money in the world would have no meaning.

~ Aristotle Onassis ~

Status of Women

Woman and teabag

A woman is like a teabag —
You can't tell how strong
she is until you put her in hot water.

~ Nancy Reagan ~

A woman's guess and man's certainty

A woman's guess is much more accurate
than a man's certainty.

~ Rudyard Kipling ~

His wife is always behind

Behind every great man is a woman,
And behind him is his wife.

~ Groucho Marx ~

Women and bachelors

Give women the vote, and in five years
there will be a crushing tax on bachelors.

~ George Bernard Shaw ~

Woman inspires but prevents

Woman inspires us to great things,
and prevents us from achieving them.

~ Alexander Dumas ~

My husband is cleverer than your husband!

Two wives were discussing about the cleverness of their husbands.

One wife was telling the other, "When my husband writes something, no one can read what he writes, only he himself can."

Then the other wife says, "I think my husband is cleverer than yours because when he writes something, he himself cannot even read it!"

One who never remembers a woman's age

A diplomat is a man who always remembers a woman's birthday but never remembers her age.

~ Robert Frost ~

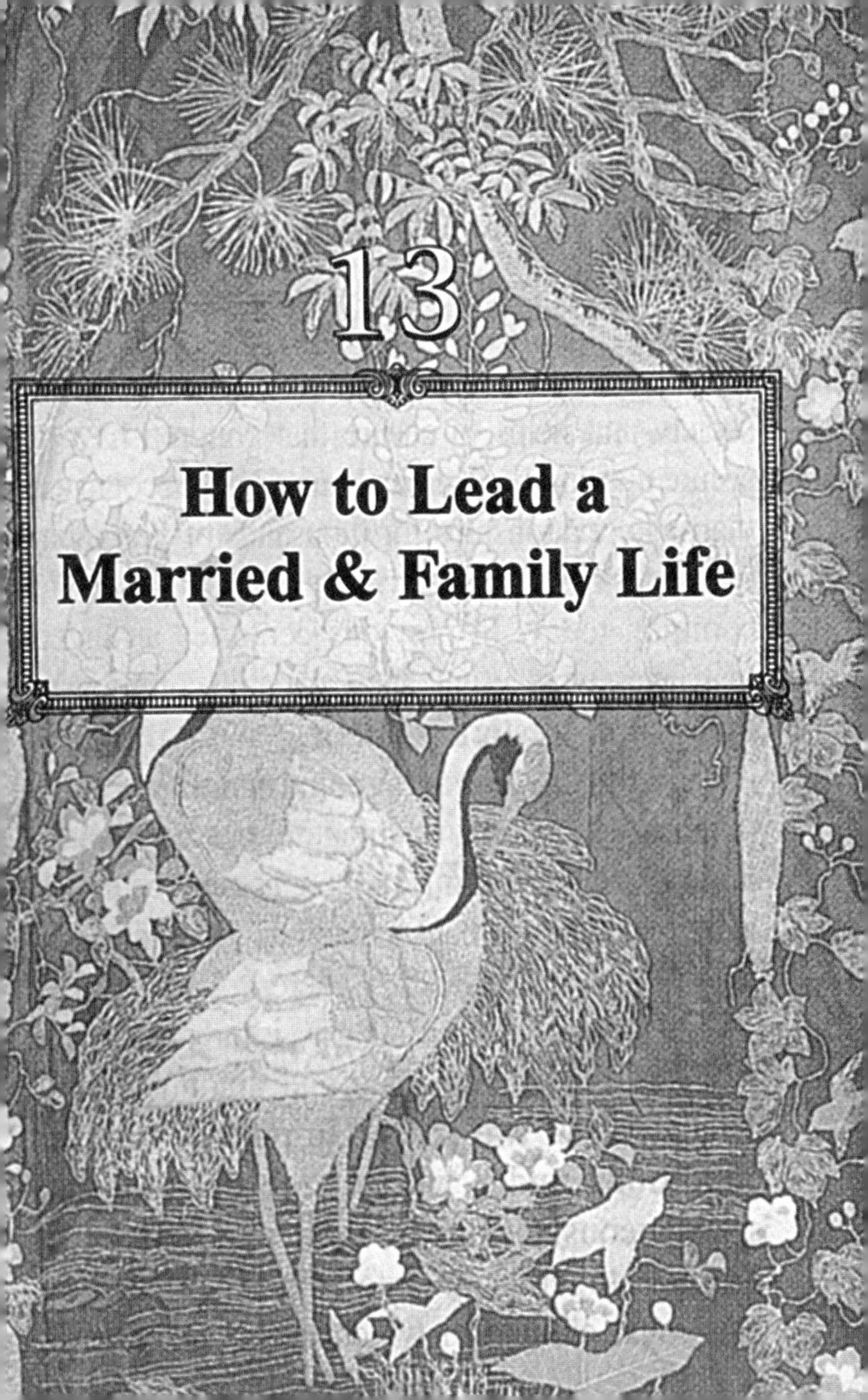
13
How to Lead a
Married & Family Life

he institution of marriage is the socially recognised union between a man and a woman that serves to legitimise their children. The official union of a man and a woman is common in every modern society and helps to ensure that children have a secure upbringing. Human beings have recognised marriage relationships for thousands of years, but marriages based on free choice and love are more common today. In previous centuries arranged marriages were usual; they are still common in many non-western societies, with relatives negotiating an advantageous match for both families. Monogamy (marriage to one person at a time) is the general rule, although some countries allow polygamy, where a man has more than one wife at a time. Polyandry, where a woman takes several husbands simultaneously, is rarer but exists.

Love is the passionate and abiding desire, on the part of two people, to produce together conditions under which each can be, and spontaneously express, their real self — to produce together an intellectual soil and an emotional climate in which each can flourish, far superior to what either could achieve alone. Marriage is one of the most fundamental and enduring social institutions.

In a true marriage, man and woman think more of the partnership than they do of themselves. It is an interweaving of interests and facing of sacrifice together for the sake of both. A feeling of security and contentment comes from mutual effort.

A family is defined as a group of persons united by the ties of marriage, or adoption, constituting a single household, and interacting with each other. Some form of family organisation is found in all human societies, although there are great variations in the type of families in different societies.

A family in the simplest terms, is the union of a man and a woman along with their offspring, usually living in a private and separate dwelling. This type of living arrangement, more specifically known as the nuclear family, is believed to be the oldest of the various types of families in existence.

What people want when they are married

A Wife needs :

Tenderness, Courtesy, Sociability, Understanding, Fairness, Loyalty, Honesty and Good companionship.

A Husband needs :

Love, Attentiveness, Family obligations, Faithfulness, Understanding, Loyalty, Proper food and to be calmed when he is in bad mood.

Marriage is a blessing

Marriage is a blessing but many people turn their married lives into a curse.

Give and take policy

Marriage is a give and take affair. The husband gives his wife everything he makes and she takes it.

~ Henry Morgan ~

(The real meaning of the give-and-take policy is to compromise.)

Blessed are those who have harmony

- Blessed are the parents and children
  who have a loving relationship among them.
- Blessed is the home
  where there is friendship and harmony.

How troubles and babies grow

Troubles and babies grow larger by nursing them.

Share the pain and pleasure

If a couple can share pain and pleasure in their day-to-day life, they can console each other and minimise their grievances.

Thus, the wife or husband should not expect to experience only pleasure in their wedded life.

Wife serves the husband in three different ways

Wife becomes a mistress to a young husband, companion to a middle-aged husband and a nurse to an old husband.

~ Francis Bacon ~

There is only one path for both

In a successful marriage, there is no such thing as one's way.

There is only the path for both, the humpy, bumpy, difficult but always-mutual path.

Woman is not a doll

A woman should not be used as a doll
in the hands of a man.

Marriage is not only for lust

Marriage for the satisfaction of mere sexual appetite is not a real human marriage but an animal act.

Woman should not be the object of man's lust

Woman must cease to consider herself the object of man's lust. The remedy is more in her hands than man's. She must refuse to adorn herself for men, including her husband, if she will be an equal partner with man.

~ Mahatma Gandhi ~

After marriage how they listen to each other

First year, wife listens to husband
Second year, husband listens to wife
Third year, neighbours listen to both of them (when they shout at each other).

Reason for divorce

Man's strange behaviour has caused the increase in the rate of divorces and many other social problems, such as uncared for children and juvenile delinquency.

Partnership is more important

In a true marriage, man and woman think more of the partnership than they do of themselves individually.

The nature of sex

There is a saying: "Like fire, sex is a good servant but a bad master."

After marriage romance ceases

When a man and woman are married their romance ceases and their history commences.

~ Rochebrune ~

Although marriage is equal partnership it is also reciprocal

Marriage is that relation between man and woman in which independence is personal and obligation is reciprocal.

~ L. K. Anspacher ~

Master and servant

Male domination has had some very unfortunate effects. It has made the most intimate of human relations that of marriage, one of master and servant, instead of one between equal partners.

~ Bertrand Russell ~

Marriage is equal to a pair of shears

Marriage resembles a pair of shears joined together so that they cannot be separated. Often they move in opposite directions.

Before marriage, a man declares he would lay down his life for her; after marriage, he won't even lay down his newspaper to talk to her.

~ Helen Rowland ~

Marriage is a gamble

Marriage is a gamble —
heads he wins, tails you lose.

Mother is the living God

People say that God could not be everywhere so he created mothers to represent him.

How to argue

When husband and wife start to argue on certain matters, one must listen, without talking, to what the other says.

When one finishes the other can start but both should not talk at the same time.

Children cherish parents' feeling

Children will not remember you for the material things you provided but for the feeling that you lavished on them.

~ Richard L. Evans ~

Something is wrong

There is something wrong about the man whose wife and children do not greet him affectionately on his homecoming.

~ Napoleon Hill ~

Nature of a child's mind

If a child fears your presence,
he will love you in absence.

Shaking hands after marriage

Shaking hands after marriage is just like the shaking of hands between two wrestlers before the fight.

Do not allow parent's heart to bleed

To lose a mother's love and care is to lose a fortune. You will realise the situation better when you are married and concerned with the doings of your own offsprings.

There is a Chinese saying, which reads, "He who causes a parent's heart to bleed shall have a child to revenge the deed."

Another person married the girl

Once a young man had fallen deeply in love with a girl from another town. He wrote long letters to her daily expressing his love for her.

After sending no less than a few hundred letters, he discovered to his horror that she had fallen in love and married the postman who had delivered the letters.

The family of success

- The father of success is work.
- The mother of success is ambition.
- The oldest son is common sense.
- Some of the other boys are:
  Perseverance, honesty, thoroughness, foresight, enthusiasm and co-operation.
- The oldest daughter is character.
- Some of her sisters are:
  Cheerfulness, loyalty, care, courtesy, economy, sincerity, and harmony.

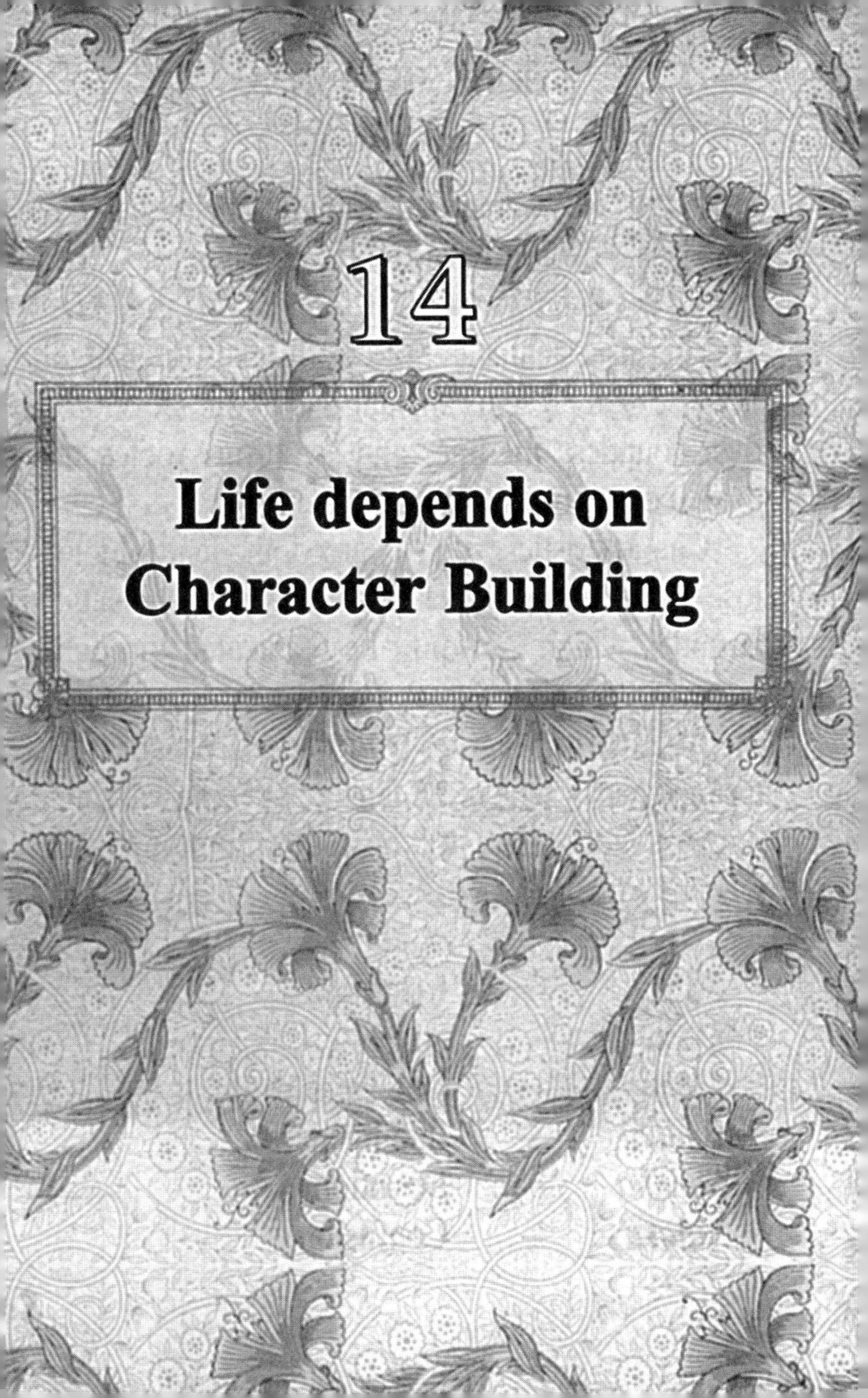

14

Life depends on Character Building

he character of a human being can be divided into two aspects the *INTRINSIC* and the *FORMULATED*. The intrinsic character is very difficult to change because it represents mental habits one develops over countless lifetimes and are firmly rooted in the subconscious mind.

Characteristics, such as greed, the tendency to lose one's temper quickly, and illwill are mental attitudes which can only be eradicated through intense effort and mental training.

According to the Buddha, there are six characteristics which humans manifest in varying degrees according to their dominant mental tendencies:

- *Raga* — Lustfulness
- *Dosa* — Anger
- *Moha* — Delusion, Dullness
- *Buddhi* — Intelligence
- *Saddha* — Devotion
- *Vittaka* — Confusion

Some of these tendencies are easily recognisable in individuals. The negative forces remain latent in the mind waiting for an opportunity to emerge, given the right circumstances.

In order to eradicate negative tendencies, one must not repress them by external behaviour or denying that they exist. It is necessary to be perfectly honest with oneself and examine oneself dispassionately, and recognise one's strength and weakness.

Once recognised, then one must go through the process of self-training. All evil thoughts must be identified, then removed from the mind, and good positive thoughts must be encouraged in their place. It is certainly not an easy task, but even at the early stages one will be surprised at the results which positive effort will bring.

A good character is the most important value that a human being can nurture. Education, experience, maturity, religious knowledge and good companions support character building.

How animals learn human monkey tricks

A family adopted a baby female chimpanzee. When this chimpanzee started to grow, the family thought that it was not nice to keep it alone and handed it over to the zoo. In that zoo, there were many wild chimpanzees. After living with them she gave birth to a baby chimpanzee but this mother chimpanzee completely neglected its young and never attended to it. However, the wild chimpanzees, which were staying there, attended to this baby and looked after it. It shows that animals, which had associated with human beings, neglect their duties and follow the human monkey tricks! Nowadays, mothers after giving birth to babies, very easily discard their babies, and run away or neglect them, but wild animals would never do that. It clearly shows in modern society that mothers can very easily neglect their humane qualities and duties.

Great people are products of courage

If you have tried and met with defeat; if you have planned and watched your plans being crushed before your eyes, just remember that the greatest men in all history were the products of courage, and courage, you know, is born in the cradle of adversity.

Honour and worthy action

True honour can only be purchased by worthy actions.

Ingredients in commitment

Faithfulness and persistence
are the first two ingredients of commitment.
Action is the third ingredient
that gives the first two lives.

Manners support virtues

Manners are the shadows of virtues.

~ Smith ~

Self-control protects everybody

If you neglect to exercise self-control,

you are not only likely to injure others, but you are sure to injure yourself!

Rise up again

Oh men, who are labelled 'failures',
rise up! Again and do!
Somewhere in the world of action is room;
there is room for you.
No failure was ever recorded,
in the annals of truthful men,
Except of the craven-hearted that fails,
nor attempts again.
The glory is in the doing,
and not in the trophy won;
The walls that are laid in darkness
may laugh to the kiss of the sun.
Oh, weary and worn and stricken,
oh, child of fate's cruel gales!
I sing — that it happily may cheer him —
I sing to the man who fails.

~ Napoleon Hill ~

Glory leads but to the grave

The boast of heraldry, the pomp of power,
And all that beauty, all that wealth ever gave,
Awaits alike the inevitable hour.
The paths of glory lead but to the grave.

~ Thomas Gray ~

Role of manners

Manners are more important than the law.

Manners open the door

Good manners will open doors
that the best education cannot.

~ Clarence Thomas ~

Manners differ

Manner is everything with some people and something with everybody.

~ Bp. Middleton ~

Mind-made world

All the actions we see in the world, all the movements in human society, all the works that we have around us, are simply the display of thought, the manifestation of the will of man.

~ Swami Vivekananda ~

No one is perfect

By nature in every man there are some good and bad habits. Nobody is perfect. The lotus flower is loved by everybody, but its stalk is thorny.

~ Hitopadesa ~

How a person became the head

The lion is regarded as the king of the beasts in the jungle although no one has appointed the lion as the king, but all animals in the jungle respects the lion as their head. It seems that, to be a head in a place the appointment is not the important thing but the person's behaviour, character and attitude are the important points.

Debt is our enemy

Debt is a merciless master,
a fatal enemy of the savings habit.

Seven social ills

- Politics without principles.
- Riches without work.
- Commerce without morality.
- Education without character.
- Pleasure without conscience.
- Science without humanity.
- Cult without sacrifice.

~ Mahatma Gandhi ~

Easy to see others' faults

It is easy to see the faults of others; but one's own is difficult to see.

One winnows other's faults like chaff; but one's own, one hides as a crafty fowler covers himself.

~ Buddha ~

Everybody makes mistakes

The only man who makes no mistakes is the man who never does anything. Do not be afraid of mistakes providing you do not make the same one twice.

~ *Roosevelt* ~

When you control yourself, you dominate your enemy

When an angry person starts to vilify and abuse you, justly or unjustly, just remember that if you retaliate in a like manner you are being drawn down to that person's mental level, therefore that person has dominated you!

On the other hand, if you refuse to become angry, if you retain your self-composure and remain calm and serene, you retain all your ordinary faculties through which to reason. You take the other fellow by surprise. You retaliate with a weapon with the use of which he is unfamiliar; consequently you easily dominate him.

~ *Napoleon Hill* ~

Life depends on Character Building

Stop being prejudiced

To live anywhere in the world and be against race, religion, colour, and traditions is like living with Eskimos in Alaska and being against snow.

No perfection without trials

A gem is not polished without rubbing,
nor is a man perfected without trials.

Mistakes become lessons

Your mistakes are new lessons for success.
If you want work well done, select a busy man — the other kind has no time.

~ Elbert Hubbard ~

Bitter criticism can cure sickness

Sweetness creates sickness; bitterness comes with the cure. Praise is sweetness, an excess of which causes sickness; and criticism is like a bitter pill, which cures. We must have the courage to welcome criticism and not be afraid of it.

Laziness is not resting
Relaxing is resting, laziness is rusting.

Conceit covers the character
Conceit is a fog, which envelops a man's real character beyond his own recognition. It weakens his native ability and strengthens all his inconsistencies.

~ Napoleon Hill ~

Strength is not in the body but in the mind
Strength does not come from physical capacity. It comes from an indomitable will.

Rise with the challenge
A kite rises against the wind, never with it.

Be firm when administering authority
Be firm when authority is required but be gentle and sweet while administering authority.

Ten kinds of duties of a ruler

- Be liberal and avoid selfishness.
  Maintain a high moral character.
  Be prepared to sacrifice one's own pleasure for the well-being of the subjects.
  Be honest and maintain absolute integrity.
- Be kind and gentle.
  Lead a simple life for the subjects to emulate.
- Be free from hatred of any kind.
  Exercise non violence.
  Practise patience.
- Respect public opinion to promote peace and harmony.

~ *Buddha* ~

First control yourself

No man can control others unless he first controls himself.

A person with well-developed self-control will never, under any circumstances, slander another person or seek revenge for any cause whatsoever.

A person with self-control will not hate

those who do not agree with him; instead, he will endeavour to understand the reason for their disagreement, and profit by it.

~ Napoleon Hill ~

Nature of a gentleman

Man must be strong enough to know when he is weak, brave enough to encounter fear, proud and unbending in honest defeat, humble and gentle in victory.

Advantage of poverty

I am thankful that I was born poor — that I did not come into this world burdened by the whims of wealthy parents, with a bag of gold around my neck.

~ Napoleon Hill ~

Sincerity brings divinity and humanity together

Sincerity is the only virtue
that binds the divinity and man as one.

In humility there is wisdom

Humility is the first sign of wisdom.

~ Booker T. Washington ~

Follow the master

If you follow the master,
the dog will never bite you.

Learn how to serve genuinely

Service without humility
is selfishness and egoism.

Learn to tolerate intolerance

The best lesson of tolerance
is to tolerate intolerance.

Be contented

I complained I had no shoes
until I met a man who had no feet.

How to be happy always

- Do not believe everything you hear;
- Do not do everything that you desire to do;
- Do not tell all you know;
- Do not use all you have;
- Do not buy everything you see;

then you will always be happy.

~ Martin Luther ~

Recall your previous problems to reduce the existing problems

Another way to reduce your problems is to recall what you have gone through before, under similar or even worse circumstances; and how you have, through your own patience, initiative and effort, been able to surmount your then seemingly insurmountable difficulties. By doing so, you will not permit your existing problems to 'drown you'.

Kindness in action rather than mere intention

To give pleasure to a single heart by a single kind act is better than a thousand heads bowing in prayer.

~ Saadi ~

Pleasant attitude fulfils other duties

You have not fulfilled every duty unless you have fulfilled that of being pleasant.

~ Charles Buxton ~

Four principles in nation building

Propriety, righteousness, integrity and a sense of

shame are the four ethical principles of nation building. Without proper development of these four ethical principles the country would face extermination.

~ Kuan Tzu ~

Something is wrong with us

The world as such is neither good nor bad. It produces criminals as well as saints, fools and enlightened ones. Out of the same clay, beautiful and ugly, useful and useless things can be made. The quality depends on the potter, not on the clay. It is not that something is wrong with the world, but something is wrong with us.

Leaders must be just and good

When the ruler of a country is just and good,
The ministers will become just and good.
When the ministers are just and good,
The officials will become just and good.
When the officials become just and good,
The people will become just and good.

~ Buddha ~

Rising when we fail

Our greatest glory isn't in never failing
but in rising every time we fail.

~ Confucius ~

It is easy to be good when everything is good but it is difficult to be good when things are bad

It may not be too difficult to do well; it is more difficult to be good.

But to maintain a good mental attitude and to do some service to others in the face of accusations, criticisms and obstructions is the most difficult of all.

Sacrifice your pride, you will find inner peace

Difficult indeed it is to subdue one's pride,
But it is advisable to reduce one's pride.
If you are able to sacrifice your pride,
Then you can find inner peace,
And experience true happiness.

Who is great in us?

Some are born great, some achieve greatness, and some hire public relations.

~ Donald Boorstin ~

Who gains victory?

He who gains a victory over other men is strong, but he who gains a victory over himself is all-powerful.

~ Lao Tze ~

Failure is our teacher

Failure is not fatal. Failure should be our teacher, not our undertaker. It should challenge us to new heights of accomplishments, not pull us to new depths of despair. From honest failure can come valuable experience.

~ William Arthur Ward ~

What life reminds us

Lives of great men all remind us.
We can make our lives sublime

And, departing, leave behind us
Footprints on the sands of time.

~ Henry Wadsworth Longfellow ~

When I am bad, everybody remembers me

- When I am good people forget me.
- When I am bad everybody remembers me.

Confidence gained through experience

Confidence comes not from always being right but from not fearing to be wrong.

~ P. J. Macintyre ~

You have to use your effort

People never get what they need, simply by thinking but by effort rightly directed.

The animals do not jump into the mouth of the lion, king of beasts who is in sleep.

~ Hitopadesa ~

Good character wins in the end

If a man has built a sound character, it makes but little difference what people say about him, because he will win in the end.

~ Napoleon Hill ~

Adversity can create good effects

A gem cannot be polished without
friction nor man perfected without adversity.

Four human characteristics

- Those who try to seek their own faults, however small these may be, try to correct these faults and only look at the good others do.
- Those who look at the good in themselves and the good in others.
- Those who only look at the good in themselves and only at the faults in others (and try to demean the one making the fault).

- Those who consider all their negative qualities as positive factors and condemn the good that others do.

~ Everyday Human Values ~

Encouraging fact

I know of no more encouraging fact than the unquestionable ability of man to elevate his life by conscious endeavour.

His candle is brighter

By blowing out the other person's candle,
one's light will burn brighter for others to see.

Criticism comes from loved ones

The apparent criticism will only be well received if it comes from someone we love or a good friend. Otherwise it is wasted and has no power to manifest positive change.

~ The Human Mind ~

Don't do it

If you don't want anyone to know,
don't do it.

~ Chinese proverb ~

Secret

Something a person tells everybody
not to tell anybody.

Leading by example

We lead first by example.
Everything we say
Or do sends a message,
Sets a tone,
Or teaches people what to do,
Or what not to do.

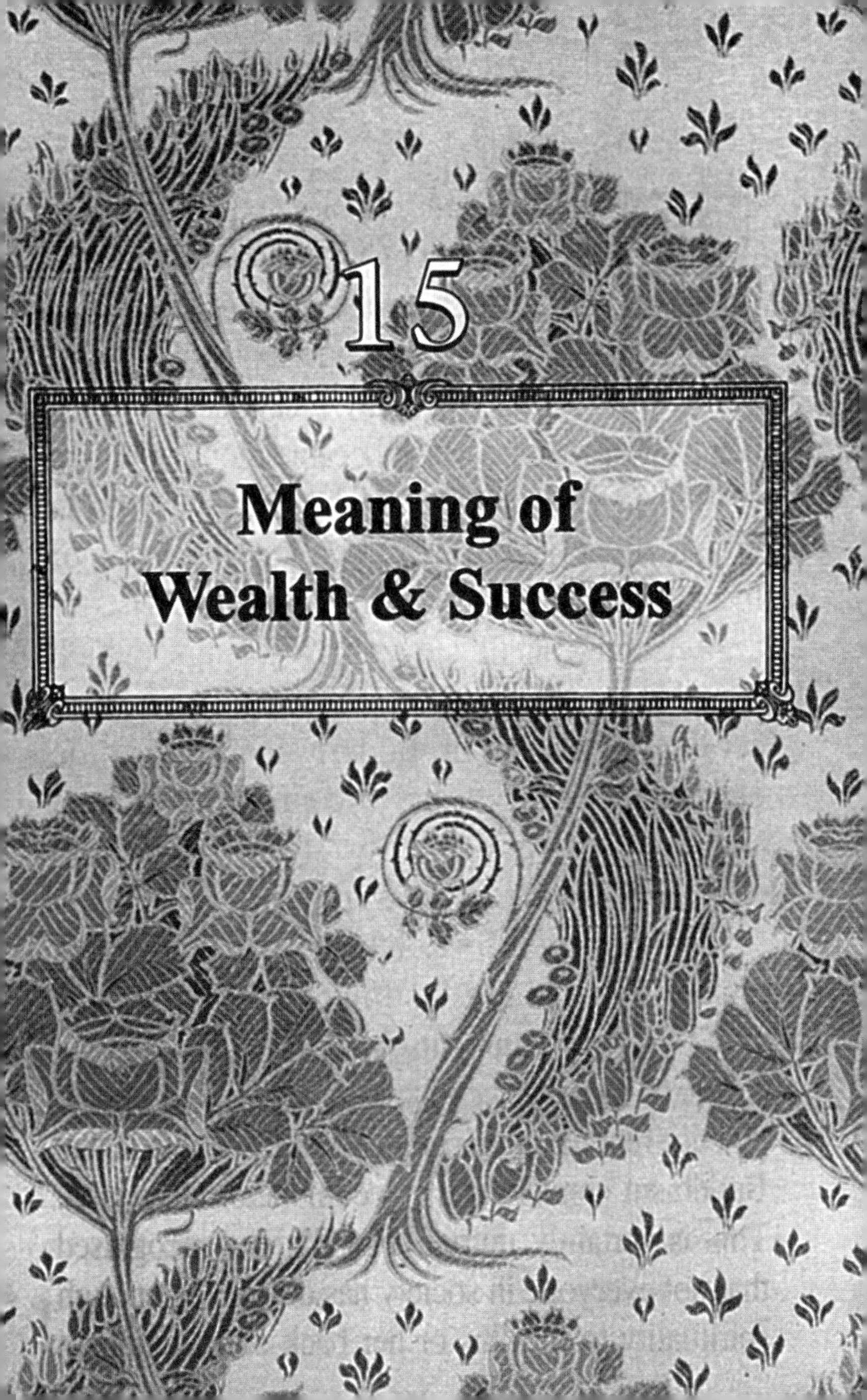

15

Meaning of Wealth & Success

o most people a wealthy person, community or nation is one that is 'well off' or 'rich' in the sense of possessing those things which contribute to material welfare. The word 'wealth' originally meant state of well being (weal) but by usage became more and more to refer to those things which generally promote physical well-being rather than the state of mental well-being itself. This wealth consists of an aggregation of substantive things, which contribute to well-being, and these things are called economic goods. In modern economies, the ownership of wealth has become more indirect and is often represented by stocks, bonds and other such instruments of ownership.

Wealth, therefore, is often thought of as consisting of these instruments, their money value, or even money itself. Because the Buddha emphasised the necessity to reduce greed and to practice renunciation, people wrongly conclude that Buddhism condemns the accumulation of wealth. This is certainly untrue. The Buddha recognised that not everyone in society has developed enough spirituality to turn his or her back on materialism and take on the life of a monk or nun. In his teaching, notably the Sigalovada Sutra and the Vyaggapaja Sutra, the Buddha gives sound advice on how wealth can be accumulated and dispensed with, to encourage charity, aid to relatives, thrift and generosity.

What Buddhism discourages however, is the total slavery to materialism. Sadly in many developed and developing societies, wealth is sought after as the ultimate goal, not as a means to promote spiritual upliftment. When a person pursues wealth at the expense of all other consideration, then it is wrong. On a national level, when governments are prepared to destroy the environment in the name of progress the citizens lose their confidence in life.

According to Buddhism wealth can be acquired, but one must use it in the service of one's family and the less fortunate beings.

Success is a related concept. We can be successful in anything we do materially. But we should never lose sight of spiritual success. Once we know that material success is subservient to spiritual progress we can seek both with understanding.

It is emphasised that we should repeat the following sentences several times daily: —

"I can be a success,
I will be a success,
I am a success."

On waking up in the morning, one should repeat these sentences several times. Before retiring at night, one should go through the routine again. These three sentences cover the three phases of success already outlined.

The thought: '**I can be a success**' is the phase of *RECOGNITION*. You recognise that you can be a success.

"**I will be a success.**" represent the phase of *REALISATION*. You realise that right thinking will bring you success – and since you are determined to think rightly, you know you will be a success. This of course applies to both material and spiritual success.

Three greatest treasures

I have just three things to teach:
Simplicity, patience, compassion.
These three are your greatest treasures.
Simple in actions and in thoughts,
You return to the source of being.
Patient with both friends and enemies,
You accord with the way things are,
Compassionate towards yourself,
You reconcile all beings in the world.

~ Lao Tze ~

Power of words

Words have the power to destroy or heal.
When words are both true and kind,
they can change our world.

~ Jack Kornfield ~

Axe in the mouth

People are born with axes in their mouths and they cut themselves with their own harsh speech.

They criticise those who should be praised and they praise those who should be criticised. The results of their behaviour comes back to them and thus they do not experience happiness.

~ Buddha - Vin ~

Wealth is neither good nor bad

Wealth is neither good nor bad,
Just as life within the world with its
sensual joys is neither good nor bad.
It depends on the way the wealth
is obtained and what is done with it,
And in what spirit it is given away.
People may acquire wealth unlawfully and
spend it selfishly.
Either case will not make one truly happy.
Instead, one can acquire wealth by lawful
means without harming others.
One can be cheerful and use wealth
without greed or lust.
One can be heedful of the dangers
of the attachment to wealth

And share the wealth with others
to perform good deeds.
One can be aware that it is not wealth
nor good deeds,
But liberation from craving and desire,
that is the goal.
In this way, this wealth brings joy and happiness
One holds wealth
not for oneself but for all beings.

~ Buddha ~

Rich man's purse and scholar's pen

The rich man takes pride in his purse,
the scholar in his pamphlets.

~ Arabic proverb ~

Ambitions never satisfy

Ambition is so powerful a passion in the human breast that however high we reach we are never satisfied.

~ Nicolo Machiavelli ~

Consider time rather than money

Money lost can be regained,
but time lost is lost forever.

The secret of success

- Occupation in work which one loves best.
- Environment where one comes in contact with others who are enthusiastic and optimistic.
- Financial success.
- Complete mastery and application, in one's daily work, of the Fifteen Laws of Success.
- Good health.
- Knowledge that one has served others in some helpful manner.
- Good clothes appropriate to the needs of one's occupation.

~ Napoleon Hill ~

An idle man is not safe

No idle person is ever safe, whether he is rich

or poor, white or black, educated or illiterate.

Immorality ruins man in five ways

He suffers from loss of wealth through his negligence (gambling, drinking, debauchery) and an evil rumour spreads about him; he does not gain confidence in whatever assembly he approaches; finally he dies with a confused mind and will be born in an unfortunate state.

~ Buddha ~

Poverty and debt are two cruel masters

Poverty, alone, is sufficient to kill off ambition, destroy self-confidence and hope, but add to it the burden of debt.

The value of a man is in his giving

The value of a man should be seen in what he gives and not in what he is able to receive.

~ Albert Einstein ~

Find the best suitable work to avoid laziness

There are no lazy men. What may appear to be a lazy man is only an unfortunate person who has not found the work for which he is best suited.

~ Napoleon Hill ~

Do what needs to be done today

The secret of happy successful living is to do what needs to be done now, and not worry about the past or the future.

We never gain through selfishness

Great achievement is usually born of great sacrifice, and is never the result of selfishness.

The devil's workshop

An idle mind is the devil's workshop.

Three ingredients for success

Service, sacrifice and self-control are three words, which must be well understood by the person who succeeds in doing something that is of help to the world.

Difference between defeat and failure

You are fortunate if you have learned the difference between temporary defeat and failure; more fortunate still, if you have learned the truth that the very seed of success is dormant in the defeat that you experienced.

Earn without harming others

Blessed are they who earn their living without harming others.

Different effects

The medicine, which cures one man's sickness,

can become a poison to another. In the same manner, one man's method for spiritual development can become a nuisance to another person.

Foolish men suffer due to their property but wise men use their wealth well.

What is a great loss?

Five kinds of loss — loss of relatives, wealth, health, morality, and right view.

No beings fall into an evil state, a hell state... after death because of loss of relatives, wealth or health; but beings do fall into such states by loss of morality and right view.

~ Buddha - D. III: 235 ~

Wealth through gambling

To seek wealth through gambling is like expecting a passing cloud to shelter us from the sun.

What can edify you?

Your wealth can only adorn your house but not you. Only your own virtue can edify you. Your dress can adorn your body but not you. Only your good conduct can.

By thinking that money can do everything, we do everything for money

Those who believe money can do everything are frequently prepared to do everything for money.

Four kinds of happiness for humanity

- Happiness gained
  through accumulation of property.
- Happiness gained
  by using one's own property to carry out the responsibilities in life.
- Happiness gained
  when one is not indebted to others.
- Happiness gained
  by leading a blameless life.

~ Buddha ~

What do you gain by expanding your wealth?

Inordinate expansion of wealth becomes not a source of happiness, but creates anxiety, and in the end, insecurity.

Through over indulgence, people destroy themselves. Many wealthy people often end up like the pitiful plight of ants, which had fallen into a cup of honey.

Silver lining in every dark cloud

Calamities are of two kinds:
misfortune to ourselves, and good fortune to others.

~ Ambrose Bierce ~

No satisfaction in wealth

Riches are like salt water — the more you drink the more you thirst.

If you want your friend to be rich, you lose him

Never pray for your friend to become wealthy for you will lose him.

~ Arabic proverb ~

Right is the winner

It is far better to be associated with a few who are right than with the mob which is wrong, because right is always the winner in the end.

~ Napoleon Hill ~

The highest achievement

Health is the highest gain
Contentment is the greatest wealth
Trustfulness is the best relative
Nirvana is the greatest happiness.

~ Buddha ~

Where is the profit?

What does it profit a man if he gains the whole world and suffers the loss of his own soul?

~ Jesus Christ ~

Failures help us to succeed

Failures are but the pillars of success.
To learn from our failures is to achieve success.
Never to have failed is never to have won.
Unless we experience failure and its bitterness,
We will never appreciate the sweetness of victory;
Failures not only help us to succeed,
They make us energetic, enthusiastic,
and rich in experience.

Wealth causes anxiety

Remember wealth gives joy only when you are young. It causes only anxiety when you reach the journey end. If you want to be happy when you are old you must spend your money upon worthy objects for the benefit of the people who need your services.

Inner conquest

- No victory is so vital,
- No achievement is so admirable,
- No triumph is so tremendous, and
- No success is so significant,
  as the inner conquest.

Train them to be useful!

They who provide much wealth for their children but neglect to improve them in virtue, do like those who feed their horses high, but never train them to be useful.

~ Socrates ~

What is right is enough

Let not that happens what we wish
but which is right.

Obstacles may help us

Without obstacles there would be
no opportunities.

Success and happiness

Success is getting what you want.
Happiness is wanting what you get.

~ W. P. Kinsella ~

Be a man of value

Try not to become a man of success,
but rather try to become a man of value.

~ Albert Einstein ~

Who is rich and who is poor?

We are rich only through what we give, and poor only through what we refuse and keep.

I take nothing

Alexander the Great, who conquered a good part of his known world, but alas not himself, is purported to have told his generals with his dying breath: "When you place me on the funeral pyre, place me with my palms facing upwards, so that all may see that though I have conquered the world I take nothing with me."

~ Everyday Human Values ~

In gain or loss, there is disappointment

Not getting what you desire, and getting what you desire can both be disappointing.

~ Jack Kornfield ~

Alms-giving contribute five things

Monks, in giving alms,
A giver gives five things to the receiver,
What five?
He gives longevity, beauty, comfort,
and strength and the power of understanding.

~ Buddha - A ~

Group decisions

Nothing is ever accomplished by a committee unless it consists of three members — one of whom happens to be sick and the other absent.

~ Hendrik Van Loon ~

Opportunities

Great opportunities come to all, but many do not know that they have met them.

The only preparation to take advantage of them is simple fidelity to what each day brings.

~ A. E. Dunning ~

Three essentials for happiness in work

In order that people may be happy in their work, three things are needed.

They must be fit for it. They must not do too much of it. And they must have a sense of success in it.

~ John Ruskin ~

16

War cannot bring Peace

ar is a violent conflict between states. Though the word is used to describe other types of conflict — civil war, class war, etc. — war is an aspect of politics. Much of man's oral and written records, perhaps as much of it as is devoted to any other human problems, deal with war. Groups of men used their hunting weapons against other men long before the dawn of history. For centuries man regarded war as an inevitable part of his fate, like his struggles with the weather, disease or the mysterious ocean.

One of the greatest novelist, Leo Tolstoy (1828 – 1910) wrote *War and Peace* in 1885 to exemplify the individual's fate by submissively performing the cruel, gloomy, irksome and in human role assigned to him by destiny.

There has not been and never will be real happiness in the world, without peace. Buddhism, above all, teaches the law of cause and effect. Peace is no exception. Peace comes primarily by the absence of war; it is a result, an end, not an instrument. It does not come by mere wishfulness or prayer. It has to be obtained by effort, by weaving the principles of righteousness into the whole fabric of human relationships.

The opposite of peace is conflict or war, which according to the Buddha, is the cause of all our unhappiness.

War is the result of tension, which is of various kinds. There are international tensions, some of which come down to us as historic legacies. We have also economic tensions between the haves and the have-nots. These manifold tensions create fear, suspicion, hatred and vindictiveness.

A man's individual life, circumstances and world are a reflection of his own thoughts and beliefs. All men are mirrors reflecting according to their own surface. All men, looking at the world of men and things, are looking into a mirror, which gives back their own reflection. It was R.L. Stevenson who once said:

" There is so much good in the worst of us,
And so much bad in the best of us,
That it ill-behoves any one of us,
To find any fault with the rest of us."

Even a rose has flaws. But why examine the flaws when you can appreciate its beauty? Bolton Hall once remarked:

" I looked at my Brother
with the Microscope of Criticism,
And I said: "How coarse my Brother is!"
I looked at him through the
Telescope of Scorn
And I said: "How small my Brother is!"
Then I looked in the Mirror of Truth
And I said: "How like me my Brother is."

Each individual lives in an individual world of his own creation. Man is false and deceitful, not merely in relation to others, but to himself as well. The remarkable thing about man is that he often deceives himself. "As we think, so we act."

"Since it is in the minds of men that wars are created, it is in the minds of men that the fortresses of peace must be erected."

War cannot bring Peace

This preamble to the UNESCO Charter reminds us that war begins in the minds of men. The Buddha made the same remark, many centuries earlier which is enshrined, in the first verse of the Dharmapada. In fact, he went much further than that; and declared that all things good and bad have their origin in the mind.

Who destroys the world?

The age old myth that many people believed for thousands of years that God or the devil can destroy this world is refuted by the realisation that man is the one who puts the world in flames and can eliminate the whole of mankind from this earth. However, still there are people on this earth who are sane enough to understand the danger that mankind is facing today.

The cause of conflict is nothing but selfish craving

Verily, due to selfish craving,
Conditioned through selfish craving,
Impelled by selfish craving,
Entirely moved by selfish craving,
Kings fight with kings,
Princes with princes,
Priests with priests,
Citizens with citizens,
Mother quarrels with son,
Son with father,
Brother quarrels with sister,

Sister with brother,
And friends quarrel with friends.
Thus thereby they suffer death or deadly pain.

~ Buddha - M. I: 86 ~

The world is an array of conflict

The world is not a coherent order but
an accidental array of conflicting forces.

~ Socrates ~

In the end there will be nobody to win the battle

The winds of the cold war are blowing all over the world. This dangerous situation can wipe out mankind from the face of the earth. In the end, there will not be anybody left in this world to win the battle.

Man's conflict is the cause of fear and worry

- Man is in conflict with nature;

- Man is in conflict with other human beings;
- Man is in conflict with himself.

So-called conquerors never succeeded in the end

Those so-called leaders in the battlefield do not realise that great conquerors of the world vanished in the course of time. There is none to shed a tear at their death.

But the great people who have conquered hearts through kindness and compassion continue to live in the minds of people and honoured as great conquerors. Some cruel leaders, who tried to achieve the aim of their lives by destroying millions of innocent people and creating disasters, never succeeded in the end.

The noblest victor

Though one should conquer a million men in the battlefield, yet he, indeed, is the noblest victor who has conquered himself.

~ Buddha - Dh. 102-103 ~

Why a man gets angry

Very often when a man is wrong and
does not admit it, he always gets angry.

Unhappiness is due to our wanting the wrong things

Buddhism teaches us that all of man's unhappiness comes from his greed for things such as pleasure that money can buy, power over other men, and, most important of all, the inherent desire to go on 'living for ever' even after one is dead. The desire of these things makes people selfish, so much so, they come to think only of themselves, to want things only for themselves, and do not, for a moment, mind what happens to other people. And since invariably they do not get all that they wish for, they become restless and discontented.

The only way to avoid this restlessness is to get rid of the selfish desires that actually cause them. This is very difficult; but when a man achieves it, he reaches a state of mind, which is the end of suffering.

The nature of man's craving

Man is never satisfied with his life. The purpose of life will elude him even after gaining the whole world.

People feel lonely when they work only for their own benefit

People are lonely because they build walls instead of bridges.

Today's physical and mental sufferings

Man is under the immense weight of present day living. Physical conditions have deteriorated to such a pathetic level that he succumbs to untimely death by peculiar types of killer diseases.

Mentally he is so tensed that he has forgotten the art of relaxing and cannot enjoy sound sleep without the aid of tranquillisers.

Do not worry about the circumstances

Buddhism teaches us not to worry about

circumstances here or hereafter, but to be concerned with our mental state, here and now. If we look after the present state of the mind, the future will look after itself.

Why worry?

For every problem under the sun
There is a remedy or there is none
If there is one try to find it
If there is none, why worry about it?

~ Santideva ~

Retaliation is not the solution

The policy of an eye for an eye will make the whole world blind.

~ Mahatma Gandhi ~

Observance of precepts supports others to live

Observance of religious principles or precepts not only benefits the one who observes them, but supports others to live peacefully. It is just as one who erects a fence or wall to protect his own house from the neighbour's house, serves to protect the neighbour's house as well.

Try to harmonise with others

If we do not know how to live up to the expectation of others, how can we expect others to live according to our expectations!

Conflict of selfish desire and worry

Buddhism says, the worries and suffering that we experience are nothing but a clash between our selfish desire and changing worldly conditions. One who develops one's mind to understand this can overcome worries and suffering.

Calmness is the nature of a cultured mind

Calmness is not weakness. A calm attitude at all times shows a man of culture.

Sensual pleasure and mental happiness

To experience sensual pleasure there must be external objects or participants but gaining mental happiness does not depend on these.

People's mentality differs

Dogs like bones, not grass, cows like grass but not bones. In the same way some people like excitement more than peace; for others, peace is more valuable than excitement.

Live in harmony

It can only come about when we live in harmony with the natural laws, which bring us health, success, contentment, and tranquillity. When we live in discord with these laws we experience sickness, failure, discontent, worry and insecurity.

Peace comes when we cope with conflicts

Peace comes not from the absence of conflict in

life but from the ability to cope with it. War is not an unavoidable law of nature.

Principles give happiness

Nothing can bring you peace but yourself; nothing can bring you peace but the triumph of principles.

~ Ralph Waldo Emerson ~

You are the cause of your happiness or unhappiness

It is not your position that makes you happy or unhappy; it is your disposition.

How important is laughter

A good hearty laugh is worth ten thousand 'groans' and a million 'sighs' in any market on earth.

~ Napoleon Hill ~

Health and hope must work together

He who has health has hope;
and he who has hope has everything.

Learn how to smile

If you can smile at life,
life will always smile at you.

Health is more important than wealth

The health of nations is more important than the wealth of nations.

~ *Will Durant* ~

Make the whole world happy

Individual happiness is conducive to the happiness of society, while the happiness of society means happiness of the nation. It is on the happiness of nations that the happiness of this world is built.

Happiness is available

Peace and happiness are possible and always available to us if we make the effort to gain them.

When mistakes arise, we need to recognise them and view things in their proper perspective.

Peace in the heart conquers opposing forces

Peace is never experienced through ill feeling. Peace is gained only by overcoming our selfishness and helping the world with acts of love. Peace in the heart conquers all opposing forces.

Contentment is the real wealth

I have great wealth that can never be taken away from me; that I can never squander; that cannot be lost by declining stocks or bad investments; I have the wealth of contentment with my lot in life.

~ Napoleon Hill ~

If you can trust yourself that is enough

If you can trust yourself when others suspect you, that is enough for you to maintain peace in your mind.

Learn to reconcile

It is so much easier to walk away from a hurtful past than to confront the issues. But we cannot remove the past from our hearts — it is there to stay. And the only hope for true peace with the past is to face it at its worst, to seek to forgive, to be forgiven, to make amends and to be reconciled.

~ Stephen Arterburn ~

War and Peace

Dr. Johan Galtung, the world-renowned authority on peace studies, has said, "Just because there is no war does not mean there is peace. Equating peace with the lack of war is like pronouncing a person healthy because there are no visible superficial signs of illness."

Laws and weapon

Laws kneel down in front of the gun.

~ Mao Zedong ~

War never solves human problems

Some people argue that conflict and war cannot be avoided because they are expressions of human nature. It is realistic enough to realise that it would be foolhardy to sit down and to do nothing when aggressors are brutally destroying innocent lives on the basis of unrealistic and unfounded claims, but we must always bear in mind that war is at best a last resort to maintain peace.

It cannot be denied that many wars being fought today are on the work of charismatic but unscrupulous leaders out to serve their own ends. They manipulate their followers to fight on their behalf, to go against the legitimate interests of the majority.

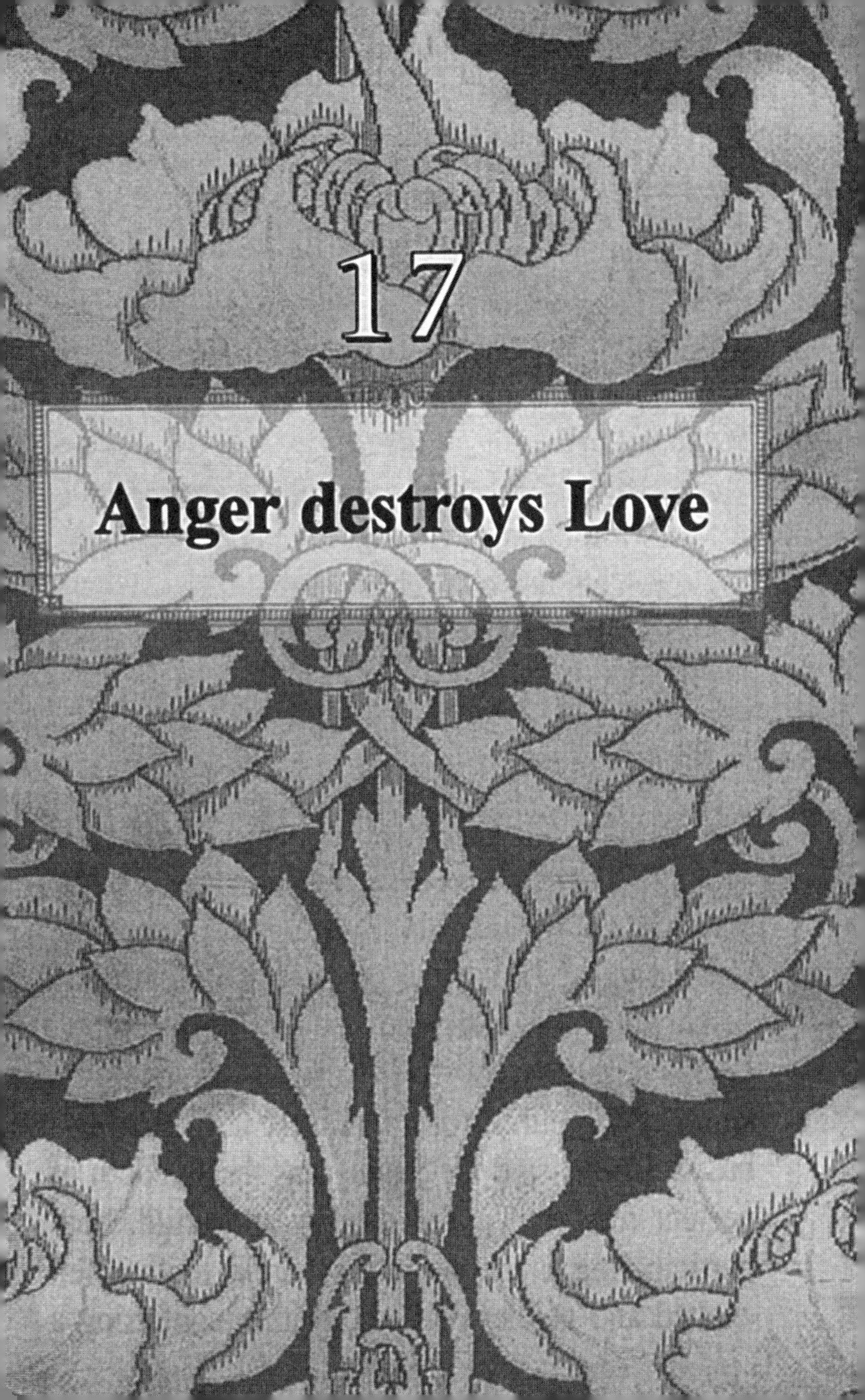

17

Anger destroys Love

ove, universal love, is the remedy for all the ills that afflict mankind. One of the most beautiful sayings about the supreme virtue of *Maitri* mentions mother-love, the foundation of all love in the world, in the *Metta Sutta* : —

> "As a mother at the risk of her life
> protects her own child,
> So also let everyone cultivate
> goodwill towards all beings."

The late Dr Ian D Suttie, in his deeply interesting and thought-provoking book, *The Origin of Love and Hate*, expressed the conclusion to which his psychological researches had brought him that the energy of human personality is a will-to-love or a will-to-fellowship. Dr Suttie saw this energy revealed in its simplest and purest form in a baby at its mother's breast. There, said Dr Suttie, was the freedom of perfect reciprocity; the mother and child, both participating in an activity wherein neither felt exalted and neither debased, neither conferring a favour nor accepting an obligation; but both alike rejoicing in the blessedness of mutual love. It is a spiritual truth that evil may only be overcome by its opposite — goodness, according to the *Dhammapada*.

Love is the antidote for hatred, and goodwill for anger; the presence of one implies the absence of the other. Anger, on the other hand, is defined as an attitude, which wants to generate violence, an agitation against something either animate or inanimate. If we look at a person, a situation or some object and do not like it and we want to express some violence and agitation towards it, to make it change in a violent way, this is a state of intolerance and a lack of patience combined with a wish to harm whatever it is that we cannot endure. Its opposite on the one hand is patience, which repels intolerance, and on the other it is love, and because love is the opposite of wishing to harm someone else. Usually we get angry at situations in which a thing happens to us which we do not like, and because they do not come up to our expectations, we get very angry with them.

Virtues beautify the body

Physical unattractiveness does not prevent one from developing a charming personality. If an ugly person cultivates the virtue of compassionate love, that love will show in so many winning ways — serenity, radiance, kindliness and gentleness.

That kind of attractiveness will easily compensate for any shortcomings in appearance. Similarly, if a handsome person cultivates hatred he transforms himself into ugliness.

A loyal heart never grows cold

Look not for beauty nor fairness of skin,
Look for a heart that is loyal within,
For beauty fades and the skin grows old,
But a loyal heart within never grows cold.

The power of kindness

Kindness is the language
which the dumb can speak,
the deaf can understand.

~ C. N. Bovee ~

Love makes home

A house is built of brick and stone
A home is made of love alone!

Four sublime nature of the mind

Metta — goodwill, compassionate love
Karuna — kindness, sympathy
Mudita — sympathetic joy without
harbouring Jealousy towards
the happiness of others.
Upekkha — equanimity or an unbiased attitude.

~ Buddha ~

How I feel when I meet another man

When I meet a man I never think of his race, colour and religion but feel that I have met another member of my human family.

~ Dalai Lama ~

How I endure abusive speech

As an elephant on the battlefield endures the arrows shot from a bow, even so, Ananda, shall I endure abusive speech; most people are, indeed, ill-natured.

~ Buddha ~

Love should complement pride

Pride makes us do things well.
But it is love that makes us do them perfectly.

The anger that you project comes back to you

By becoming angry one is like a man throwing dust against the wind — he only soils himself. For it was said by the Buddha that:

"When a fool hates a man who is free from hate,
Who is purified and free from every blemish,
Such evil he will find comes back on him;
As does fine dust blown up against the wind."

Anger destroys Love

People love beauty of a woman more than virtues of a man

I have never seen anyone who can love virtue in man as much as he loves beauty in woman.

Start your love after a second look

Love at first sight is possible,
but it is always good to take a second look.

Loose talk comes from wine

When wine sinks, words swim.

Danger of jealousy

Jealousy is a deadly poison.

How bottle takes the man

First, man takes a bottle,
After that, the bottle takes another bottle,
Later, bottle takes the man.

Anger is ugly

How ugly is the angry man!
His sleep is without comfort;
Despite his wealth he is always poor.
Filled by anger as he is,
He wounds by acts of body and speech.

~ Buddha - A. I: 3 ~

Mother's real love and tragic incident

A mother and her infant child were visitors at a zoo. Whilst on their rounds they came to a deep enclosure where lions were confined below.

As the mother and child had already spent a considerable time on their rounds at the zoo, the child became tired, agitated and restless. This resulted in the mother inadvertently losing her hold on the struggling baby. The child fell off from the mother into the deep enclosure of the lions.

Remorse stricken, the alarmed mother, with only the thought of the child uppermost on her mind, plunged herself down, without any hesitation, into the depths of the enclosure.

Needless to say, both mother and child were savagely mauled by the marauding lions. This incident shows the intrinsic and affectionate love of a mother that she is willing to sacrifice even her life for the sake of her child.

When anger is killed, all our enemies are killed

How many evil men could I kill?
Their number is boundless as the sky.
But if the thought of anger is killed,
all enemies are killed.

~ Shatideva ~

Suspicion destroys love

At the gate at which suspicion enters,
love goes out.

~ Thomas Fuller ~

One who is blind always

Certain creatures cannot see in the daytime

while others in the dark at night.
But a person who harbours hatred does not see or perceive anything, either day or night.

Anger burns us

The stronger the anger,
the stronger we burn.
It is a very painful sensation.

~ Bhikkhu Visuddhacara ~

The man who has no one

Proud man hath no God
The envious man hath no neighbour
An angry man hath not even himself.

~ Hall ~

Observing others' faults disturbs your own mind

He who is always observant of others' faults, and is irritable, his own defilements increased.

He is far from the destruction of defilement.

~ Buddha - Dh. ~

Envy is like sand in your eye

The torment of envy is like a grain of sand in the eye.

To cultivate our values

Never reprimand the errors of others;
never expose the personal affairs of others;
Never remember past bad relations with others;
With these we can cultivate our values and avoid disasters.

~ Hong Tze Tzen ~

You yourself suffer from anger

By being angry with another, you may or may not make him suffer, but you are certainly suffering now.

~ Bhikkhu Visuddhacara ~

To escape sorrow

If you are patient in one moment of anger,
you will escape a hundred days of sorrow.

~ Chinese proverb ~

You lose your happiness

For every minute you are angry,
you lose sixty seconds of happiness.

~ Ralph Waldo Emerson ~

Angry man leads a miserable life

Anger makes our life miserable. If we continue to accept anger and make no great effort to curb it, we will continue to live turbulent lives.

~ Bhikkhu Visuddhacara ~

Slay anger

Slay anger and you will be happy, slay anger and you will not sorrow.

For the slaying of anger in all its forms with its poisoned root and sweet sting — that is the slaying the nobles praise; with anger slained, one weeps no more.

~ Buddha ~

Hate bites ourselves

It is said that a rattlesnake, if cornered, will become so angry it will bite itself. That is exactly what the harbouring of hate and resentment against others is — a biting of oneself.

We think we are harming others in holding these spites and hates, but the deeper harm is to ourselves.

~ E. Stanley Jones ~

Hatred is only overcome by love

Darkness cannot be dispelled by darkness
But by brightness
Hatred cannot be overcome by hatred
But by loving kindness.

~ Buddha – Dh. ~

Unhealthy emotions create bodily sickness

Besides being poison to our mind, anger and hatred are also a danger to our physical health.

Medical science has confirmed that anger and other unhealthy emotions can contribute to bodily disease.

~ Bhikkhu Visuddhacara ~

How to overcome negative aspects

Let us overcome the angry man with gentleness,
The evil man with goodness.
The miser with generosity.
The liar with truth.

~ Buddha ~

Love their mother

The most important thing a father
can do for his children is to love their mother.

~ Theodore M. Hasburgh ~

Happy is he who makes others happy

- Happy is he who has lofty and noble aspirations
- Happy is he who enriches the lives of others
- Happy is he who allows others to live in peace
- Happy is he who makes this world a better place to live in.
- Happy is he whose work, chores and daily tasks are labours of love.
- Happy is he who loves love.

We are a reflection of our thoughts and actions

The world is like a mirror
If we look at it with a smiling face,
We see the face smiling back at us
But if we look at it with a face of anger,
We will see an ugly face reflected back.
In the same way, if we act with
kindness and compassion,
We will reap the same good qualities.

Joy of a mother

No joy in nature
Is so sublimely affecting
As the joy of a mother
At the good fortune of her child.

~ Jean Paul Richter ~

Love is life

Scientists tell us that without the presence
Of the cohesive force amongst atoms
That comprises this globe of ours,
It would crumble to pieces and
we will cease to exist;
And, even, as there is a cohesive force
in blind matter,
So must there be in all things animate:
And the name for that cohesive force
Among animate things is Love.
Where there is Love....
There is life;
Hatred leads to destruction.

~ Mahatma Gandhi ~

Anger destroys Love

Love is unstable

When poverty knocks at the door,
love flies through the window.

Love is blind

In spite of love being blind,
most men prefer to propose in the dark.

What should we give?

You give but little
when you give your possessions.
It is when you give of yourself
that you truly give.

To gain happiness do not disturb others' happiness

One can't gain happiness by destroying others' happiness, but by giving happiness and peace to others.

~ *Everyday Human Values* ~

No taste!

Eating rice and curry by fork and spoon is like making love through an interpreter!

~ Indian saying ~

Nothing worse than anger

Anger can ruin all good practices and it is not soon forgotten. It is attractive neither in the present nor when viewed later as something belonging to the past.

When anger begins burning out of control like a raging fire, protect yourself and do not let it consume you. Like a thief this fire will take away everything you have. There is nothing worse than anger.

~ Sutra of Bequeathed Teachings ~

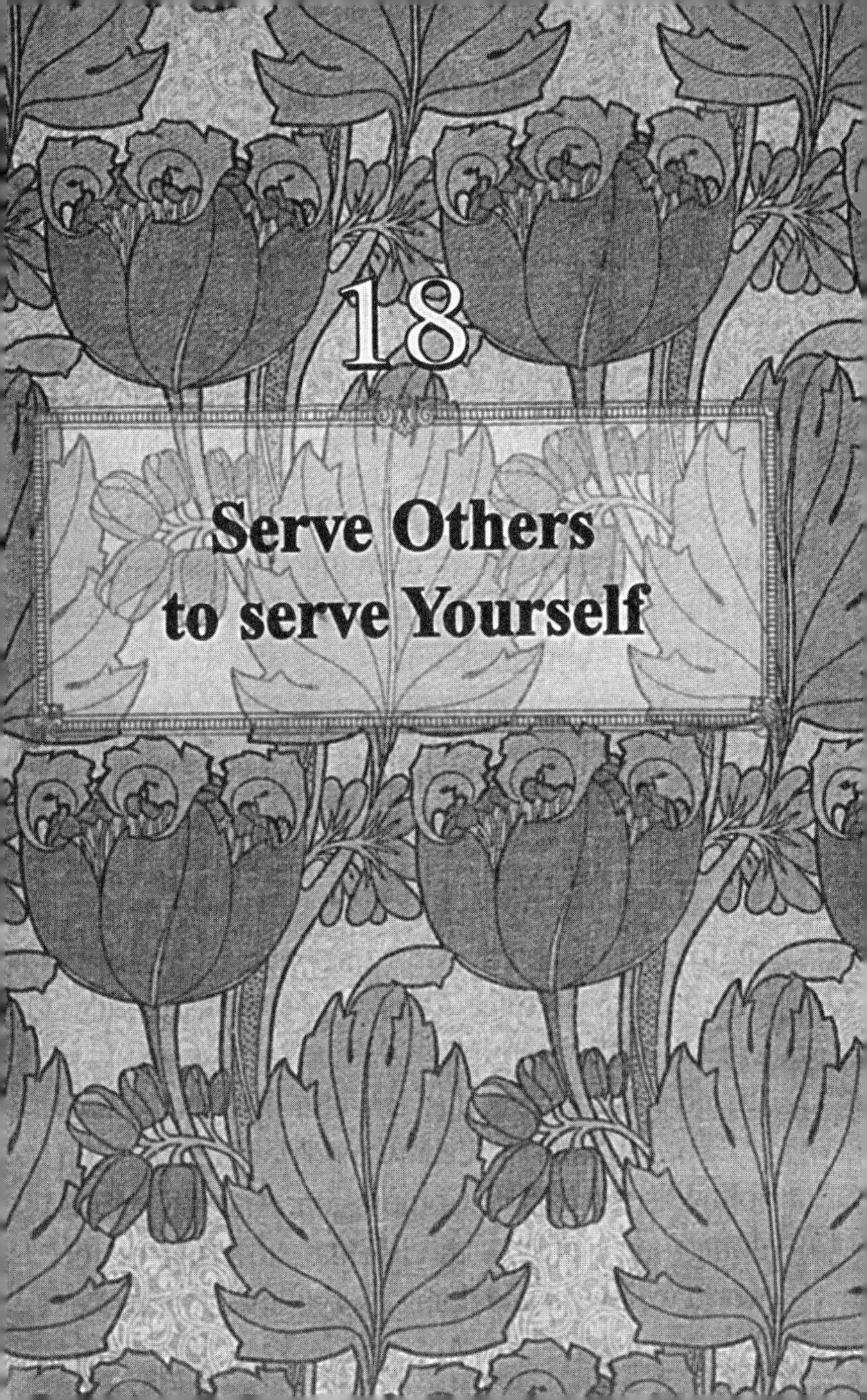

18

Serve Others to serve Yourself

hen we consider the three great questions, Who am I? What am I doing here? Am I needed? The answer to the third question will truthfully be that we are really not needed. How many great people who did so much for humanity have died? And did the world stop just because of that? Of course not. We mourned Martin Luther King, J. F. Kennedy, Mahatma Gandhi and Mother Theresa but we continued living as before.

However, the great thing about these people is that they never worried about whether they were needed or not, that was not important. What was important was that they made themselves needed at least for as long as they were alive. We too can make ourselves needed and make our lives meaningful if only we are prepared to serve others. A life lived in the service of humankind is the only worthwhile life that can be lived.

For Buddhists, the most noble path one can follow is the path of Compassion. And this means doing one's utmost to ease the suffering of the world we live in and doing everything in our power to reduce that suffering in others. It was to serve all living beings that the Buddha, motivated by boundless compassion, strove for forty-five years to spread his sublime message to bring happiness to all creatures that are born.

There are many ways to serve. We can introduce noble religious principles to help people to gain knowledge and wisdom, we can spread fearlessness by giving courage to others who are led by ignorance, we can give material things, we can give our time and energy. There is no one in the world who cannot be of some service to others. The challenge is for us to find what our strengths are and use them without any expectation of reward. It is only by spreading happiness selflessly that we can be truly happy ourselves.

Compensation of helping

It is one of the most beautiful compensations of this life that no man can sincerely try to help another without helping himself.

A teacher's attitude towards his disciples

A Buddhist monk once had two disciples; one was intelligent and attended to his duties, whilst the other was dull and kept mostly to himself as he was incapable of contributing anything useful.

In the course of time, the intelligent disciple who was frustrated approached the teacher and asked the teacher to send the other disciple away, or otherwise he would leave the place himself.

The teacher's reply to the intelligent disciple was that, "In view of your talent, you can manage to survive and others will welcome you. If you go away from this place, I do not worry about you. As to the other disciple, he will not be able to fend for himself, or survive on his own, nor can he expect any sympathy from the public, and hence he needs to be sheltered for his own safety and survival."

Why wait for gratitude?

If we want to find happiness, let us stop thinking about gratitude or ingratitude and give for the inner joy of giving.

Ingratitude is natural — like weeds. Gratitude is like a rose. It has to be fed, watered and cultivated, loved and protected.

One who works for the benefit of others also works for himself

The man who works for others
without any selfish motive,
really does good to himself.

~ Sri Ramakrishna ~

When we reduce selfishness, we become useful to others

When we stop thinking only of our own benefit, we become important to others.

Everyone needs to be valued

- Everyone needs to be valued.
- Everyone has the potential to give something back.

~ Princess of Wales, Diana ~

One who is good to himself is good to everybody

If you are good to yourself, you are good to others. If you are good to others, you are good to yourself.

If we do not serve living ones how can we serve the dead?

We cannot as yet do our duties to living men, how can we hope to serve the spirits of the dead?

~ Confucius ~

Three satisfactions

Gods are satisfied when sacrifices are performed.

Serve Others to serve Yourself

Ancestors are satisfied when offsprings remain.
Sages are satisfied when knowledge is transmitted.

~ Mencius ~

Poverty and eating less

To recommend thrift to the poor
is like advising a man who is starving to eat less.

~ Oscar Wilde ~

Help the weak if you are strong

Help the weak if you are strong
Love the old if you are young
Own a fault if you are wrong
Forgive the other if he is wrong.

Wisdom, skill and service

- To know what to do is wisdom;
- To know how to do is skill;
  But doing it as it should be done is service.

Real service

Never talk about supernatural powers and spirits, How can we serve the ghosts if we cannot serve the human beings?

The real significance of serving the people is to avoid all sorts of ghosts and spirits.

~ Confucius ~

Do some service to others

Main purpose of life is to do some service to others for their well being.

When we serve others, naturally we serve ourselves.

Help is better than preaching

When a person is down in the world, an ounce of help is better than a pound of preaching.

~ Bulwer ~

Honesty is very rare

To be honest, as this world goes,
is to be one man picked out of ten thousand.

~ Shakespeare ~

Only he himself knows his honesty

To one who said, "I do not believe that there is an honest man in the world,"
Another replied, "It is impossible that any one man should know all the world,
but quite possible that one may know oneself."

Body is a temple

There is but one temple in the world,
And that is the body of man. —
Nothing is holier than this high form. —
We touch heaven when we lay our hand on a human body.

~ Novalis ~

Humility measures our value

Humility is to make a right estimate of one's self.

~ Spurgeon ~

Place for humility in religion

Should you ask me,
What is the first thing in religion?
I should reply,
The first, second, and third thing therein — nay,
All — is humility.

~ St. Augustine ~

Humility never deprives us

Humility is not a weak and timid quality;
It must be carefully distinguished
From a grovelling spirit. —
There is such a thing as an honest pride and self-respect. —
Though we may be servants of all,
We should be servile to none.

~ E. H. Chapin ~

Who takes the fees?

God heals, and the doctor takes the fees.

~ Franklin ~

Respect begets respect

Respect is an important ingredient in life.
If we do not respect others
We may not treat them well.
Everyone deserves respect and
To be treated well.

~ Lessons in Enlightenment ~

Keep doing good

Keep doing good deeds long enough, and you'll probably turn out a good man in spite of yourself.

~ Louis Auchincloss ~

Where is the value of life

One's life has value so long as one attributes value to the life of others, by means of love, friendship, indignation and compassion.

~ Simone De Beauvoir ~

Do not expect anything in return

- Do everything with a mind that lets go.
- Do not expect praise or reward.

~ Achaan Chah ~

Service is better than rule

The high destiny of the individual is
to serve rather than to rule...

~ Albert Einstein ~

Always think of other's welfare

Be unselfish. That is the first and final commandment for those who would be useful and happy in their usefulness.

If you think of yourself only, you cannot develop because you are choking the source of development, which is spiritual expansion through thought for others.

~ Charles W. Eliot ~

What we have done for others become immortal

What we have done for ourselves alone dies with us; what we have done for others and the world remains and is immortal.

~ Albert Pike ~

Lift up others

If you want to lift yourself up,
lift up someone else.

~ Booker T. Washington ~

Find yourself to lose yourself

The best way to find yourself is to lose yourself in the service of others.

~ Mahatma Gandhi ~

Highest form of self-interest

Human service is the highest form of self-interest for the person who serves.

~ Elbert Hubbard ~

Good services will be remembered

Sow good services:
Sweet remembrances will grow from them.

~ Germaine De Stael ~

Live for others

He who lives not to others,
lives little to himself.

~ Michel Eyquem De Montaigne ~

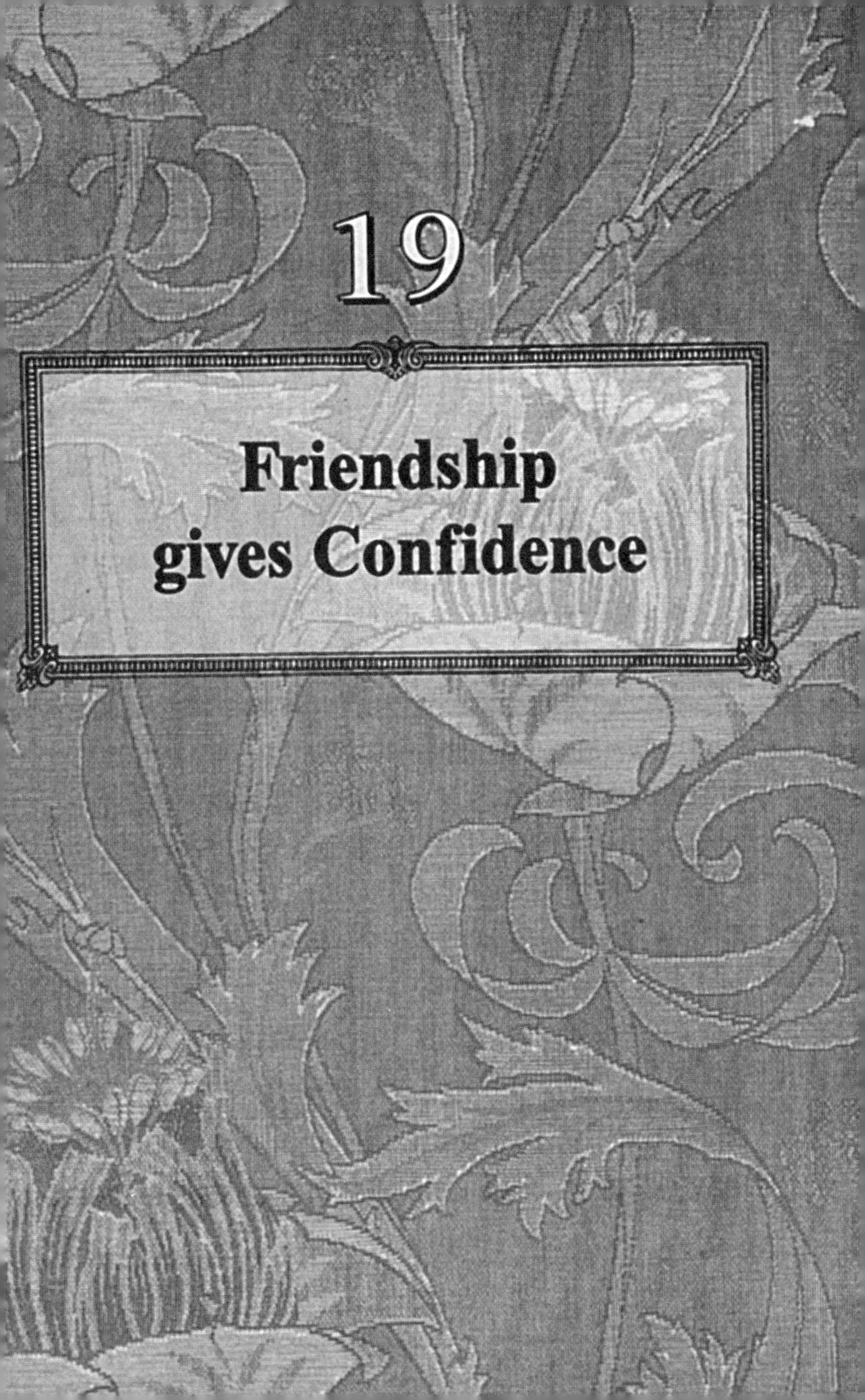

19

Friendship gives Confidence

eople typically consider friendship a voluntary or freely chosen relationship. This is in contrast to family, who are not freely chosen, or interactions with people at work which are not voluntary. Humans are by nature social beings. But this is not by choice; it is a matter of survival. These friendly interactions make people feel that their presence is valued. Friendship is seen as an equity relationship, where the norm is that what a friend does for you needs to be reciprocated in some form as gratitude.

Spending time together means that friends seek out each other's company. Nevertheless, while friends wish to spend time together, friendship is typically not experienced as exclusive, such as romantic relationship. Companionship, on the other hand, means having someone to do and share things with and to be of service in times of need. This is an obvious benefit of friendship. Emotional support from friends often takes the form of gratitude, moral support, and may occur in both mundane and crisis situations.

Friendship gives Confidence

Some friendships are of long duration, while others are relatively brief. Research has found that two-thirds of older persons have had friendships that lasted throughout their life.

As people age, their needs for social support may increase as they are confronted with mobility, health and stamina difficulties. At the same time, the death and retirement, movements of friends may reduce the size of their social network. Having friends seems to make a diffeence in people's lives. It may foster self-esteem, providing services to the needy, promoting social competence and inhibit loneliness.

According to the Buddha, we must seek out good spiritual friends who will support us as we strive to attain perfection. These friends will point out our weakness without rancour and encourage us in our practice of the Buddha's teachings. Friends like these do not expect anything in return and are only concerned with our welfare. We in return treat them in the same way and we work for our mutual benefit.

The nature of friend

There are four kinds of friends,
This you must know.
One is like a flower, another like a scale.
One like a mountain and one like the earth.

~ Fo Shuo Pei Sutra ~

Hate opens the gate to degeneration

To the man who has begun to hate himself, the gate to degeneration has already opened, and the same is true of a nation.

~ Swami Vivekananda ~

The root of civilisation is in morality

The tree of civilisation has its roots in moral values which most of us do not realise.

Without these roots, the leaves would fall and the tree will remain as a lifeless stump.

What has happened to human sympathy?

Never before in human history has mankind reached the brink of total destruction through the use of lethal nuclear weapons.

Peace-loving innocent people worry deeply over the deterioration of human sympathy and understanding. They are watching and sighing with great alarm.

One who is good to strangers is a citizen of the world

If a man is gracious and courteous to strangers it shows he is a citizen of the world.

Must have sympathy irrespective of religions

When they came to harm the Christians,
I did nothing because I was not a Christian.
When they came to harm the Hindus,
I did nothing because I was not a Hindu.

When they came to harm the Atheist,
I did nothing because I was not an Atheist.
When they came to harm the Muslims,
I did nothing because I was not a Muslim.
When they came to harm me, there was nobody left to protect me.

The difference between East and West

- Eastern man is intuitive
  Western man is intellectual
- Eastern man is lethargic
  Western man is active
- Eastern man is spiritual
  Western man is materialistic
- Eastern man is mystical
  Western man is ethical
- Eastern man is introvert
  Western man is extrovert
- Eastern man is contented
  Western man is discontented and craves for more.

~ Dr. Radhakrishnan ~

How to take a guide

- I take as my guide the hope of a saint:
- In crucial things, unity...
- In important things, diversity...
- In all things, generosity

~ George Bush ~

Give in return as much as is received

Many times a day, I realise how much my own outer and inner life is built upon the labours of my fellow men, both living and dead, and how earnestly I must exert myself in order to give in return as much as I have received.

~ Albert Einstein ~

Where joy is shared and sorrows eased

- Where joy is shared and sorrows eased,
- Where fathers and mothers
  are respected and loved,
- Where children are wanted,
- Where the simplest food is good

enough for kings because it is earned,
- Where money is not so important as loving-kindness,
- Where even the tea-kettle sings for happiness, that is home, God blesses it.

Do not break friendship

Break not the friendship of a friend in vain:
The same friendship you will never regain,
For friendship once broken like a china bowl
Can never, never again be made whole.
It can be mended like the china bowl;
it's true, but the parts mended
will always remain in view.

Be grateful

Do not kick the ladder, after climbing the roof.

A reliable friend gives confidence

Life has no blessing like a prudent friend.

~ Euripides ~

Friendship gives Confidence

Man is afraid of man

In earlier days, man was afraid of wild animals and devils, so he carried weapons for his protection.

Today, man is not very much afraid of them because he knows how to overcome them. He is afraid of human beings, because he does not know how to deal with them. So, he has to carry weapons to protect himself from his own kind.

When do I feel loneliness?

When I am alone, I do not feel loneliness because I have freedom.

When I am in the society with others, I feel loneliness because of various forms of discrimination and the manners and traditions that I have to follow.

A true friend

A true friend is one who knows all your faults, and still loves you.

How to shake hands?

You cannot shake hands with a clenched fist.

~ Indira Gandhi ~

Real friendship

There can be no friendship without confidence and no confidence without integrity.

~ Samuel Johnson ~

How friendship supports us

Friendship improves happiness and abates misery, by the doubling of our joy and the dividing of our grief.

~ Bacon ~

Never let him know too much

Have a friend and trust him such,
Never let him know too much
For if that friend becomes a foe,
Then all your secrets the world will know.

Friendship gives Confidence

New and old friends

Make new friends but keep the old,
The first is silver but the latter gold.

Silence is a friend

Silence is a friend that will never betray you.

~ Confucius ~

With whom you dare to be yourself

What is a friend? I will tell you.
It is a person with whom
you dare to be yourself.

~ Frank Crane ~

A prayer

Lord, save me from my friends.
I know how to protect myself
from my enemies.

~ Voltaire ~

Allow others to share your happiness

Men of the noblest dispositions think themselves happiest when others share their happiness with them.

The art of criticism

To be criticised is not necessarily to be wrong.

~ Sir Anthony Eden ~

Where is wisdom?

- There's wisdom
  in taking the time to care.
- There's wisdom in giving
  and wanting to share.
- There's wisdom in grace
  and making amends.
- There's wisdom in having
  and keeping good friends.

No language for friendship

The language of friendship is not words,
but meanings.
It is intelligence above language.

~ Thoreau ~

The ornament of a house

The ornament of a house is the friend
who frequents it.

~ Emerson ~

The choice is difficult

The difficulty in life is the choice.

~ George Moore ~

Friendship is for everything

By friendship you mean the greatest love, the greatest usefulness, the most open communication, the noblest sufferings, the severest truth, the heartiest counsel, and the greatest union of minds of which brave men and women are capable.

~ Jeremy Taylor ~

False friends and true friends

False friendship, like the ivy, decays and ruins the walls it embraces; but true friendship gives new life and animation to the object it supports.

~ Burton ~

Virtuous friends

Friendship must be accompanied with virtue, and always lodged in great and generous minds.

~ Trap ~

Friendship grows slowly

Friendship is a plant of slow growth, and must undergo and withstand the shocks of adversity before it is entitled to the appellation.

~ Washington ~

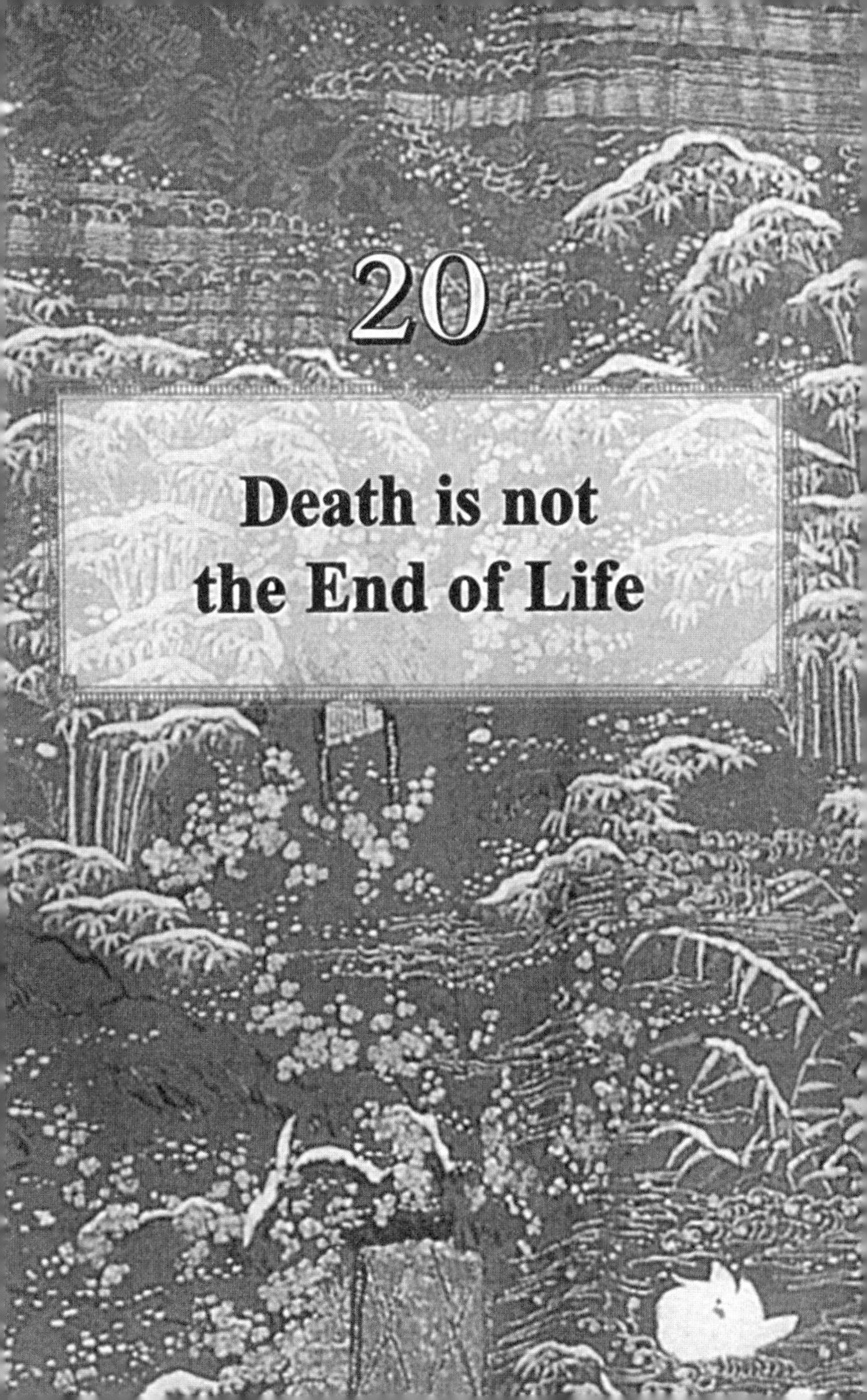

20

Death is not the End of Life

eath is the cessation of life processes that eventually occurs in all-living organisms. The state of death has always been obscured by mystery and superstition. The precise definition of human death remains controversial and differs according to traditional beliefs.

Human beings have more fear on death. They also cannot understand that one day they have to face death. That is why they worry unnecessarily about it. Worrying about it will not make death go away, so why not accept it calmly? Death comes to all; some die in their prime, others in old age, but all must inevitably die. Uninvited we come into this world and unbidden we leave it.

We know not whence we come nor whither we shall go, as we leave the world, we go forth into the darkness, naked and alone. Kith and kin, friends and relations can accompany the dead man up to his grave but not further. Only his deeds, good or bad go forth with him. However, death is not the end of a life.

Death is not the End of a Life

Death comes to all and is part of our life cycle. Inevitably I am going to die — so does everybody, every plant, every form, every living being, which follows the same path. Soon it will be autumn, the leaves will fall off the trees. We do not cry, it is natural that is what the leaves are supposed to do at the end of the season. Human beings experience the same thing.

Religious people usually have less fear of death than very materialistic people, because materialists are particularly interested only in this life to satisfy their senses and developing their attachment towards their property.

Death is universal and it strikes all and spares none. Sorrow is the heritage of everyone. The Buddha explained that death is to be expected as a natural phenomenon in all living beings.

No death without birth

One day the Buddha advised Ananda, "If anybody should ask the question as to why death takes place, tell them that death takes place because of birth. If there is no birth then there is no death. If you try to prevent death by force, then you do not understand nature. You are in fact going against the laws of nature."

The setting sun in one country becomes the rising sun in another country. So a setting sun is not the end of the sun. In the same manner, death itself is not the end of a life.

Death is the beginning of a life. Birth brings the death certificate. So if we want to avoid death, we must prevent birth.

Do something for others

Death is no cause for sorrow, but it would be sorrow if one dies without having done something for oneself and for the world.

What dies?

- Old photographers never die;
  they just stop developing,
- Old accountants never die;
  they just lose their balance,
- Old lawyers never die;
  they just lose their appeal,
- Old professors never die;
  they just lose their faculties.

Nothing to bring and nothing to take away

At birth we bring nothing;
at death we take nothing away.

~ Chinese proverb ~

Death is a rhythm of nature

Death is not unique event in our progress. It is part of a continually recurring rhythm of nature, making a crisis in the history of the individual.

~ Dr. Radhakrishnan ~

Live well to die well

For any human being, next to living well is the importance of dying well.

We carry only good deeds and bad deeds

We know not whence we come nor whither we shall go, as we leave the world; we go forth into the darkness, naked and alone. Kith and kin, friends and relatives can accompany the dead man up to his grave but not further. Only his deeds, good or bad, go forth with him.

A hero dies only once

Cowards die many times before their deaths,
The valiant never tastes of death but once.

~ William Shakespeare ~

Samsara – the repeated birth and death

The constant succession of birth and death of each individual life-flux is technically known as *samsara*. *Samsara* is the recurrent wandering of the life-flux in the ocean of birth and death.

This life-stream or *samsara* flows *ad infinitum*, as long as the muddy waters of ignorance and craving feed it. When these two are completely cut off, then only does the life-stream cease to flow; then rebirth ends, as in the case of Buddha's and Arahants'. The ultimate beginning of this life-stream cannot be determined, as a stage cannot be perceived when this life force was not fraught with ignorance and craving.

The rounds of rebirths or *samsara* do not automatically come to an end. Nor is there any point at which all beings revolving in *samsara*, gain their release by reason of its ceasing, for it has no temporal boundaries.

To run away from death

Struggle for survival means
trying to run away from death.
There is no life without death and
there is no death without life.

Life without death can be a burden

If there were no death, life would become stagnant, monotonous, unspeakably burdensome and boring.

If man were given the insight to realise and know the time of his death, he would definitely act differently from what he is doing presently. Death is only physiological erosion of the human body.

In memory of the departed

When Prophet Mohammed was asked what one must do in memory of departed parents, he advised the questioner to dig a well for people to drink water to quench their thirst.

Why be afraid of death?

The world is afraid of death,
To me it brings happiness.

~ Guru Nanak ~

Why fear death?

To be afraid of dying is like being afraid of discarding an old worn-out garment.

As long as there is fear of death, life itself is not being lived to its fullest and at its best.

No self to die

We are all a combination of mind and matter and as such there is actually no individual self to die.

Name never dies

Man's body turns to dust,
but his name or influence persists.

~ Buddha ~

Birth, death, rebirth

In brief, the combination of mind and matter is called birth. Existence of these two groups as a bundle is called life. Dissolution of these two is called death. And recombination of these two is called rebirth.

Nobody returned to tell us

Strange, is it not, that of the myriad who
Before us passed the door of darkness through,
Not one returns to tell us of the road
Which to discover we must travel too.

~ Omar Khayyam ~

Learn how to die better

To every man upon this earth
Death cometh soon or late.
And how can men die better
Than facing fearful odds,
For the ashes of his fathers,
And the temples of his Gods?

~ Lord Macaulay ~

Fear breeds death

Of all the wonders that I yet have heard.
It seems to me most strange.
That man should fear, seeing that death.
A necessary end will come when it will come.

~ William Shakespeare ~

What we received after our death

A rich man, prior to his death, bequeathed $100,000 each to three persons, namely his doctor, his priest and his lawyer, on the understanding that at the funeral ceremony each of them should deposit the allotted sum into the coffin before burial takes place.

The doctor announced that he had deducted $25,000 being amount of medical bills due to him and that he had deposited the remaining balance into the coffin.

The priest also said that he had to deduct $30,000 on account of roof repairs to his place of worship and only the balance he had placed in the coffin.

The lawyer said that he was acting according to the law and accused the other two persons for disappointing the deceased. He accordingly deposited his entire $100,000 allotted to him, plus the total amounts spent by the other two, but in the form of an Account Payee Cash cheque, which he placed into the coffin.

Life after death is not a mystery

The difference between death and birth is only a thought-moment: the last thought-moment in this life conditions the first thought-moment in the so-called next life, which, in fact, is the continuity of the same series.

During this life itself, too, one thought-moment conditions the next thought-moment. So, from the Buddhist point of view, the question of life after death is not a great mystery, and a Buddhist is never worried about this problem.

~ Ven. Dr. W. Rahula ~

List of Abbreviations

A	*Anguttara Nikaya*
Dig	*Digha Nikaya*
Dh	*Dhammapada*
Dhs	*Dhammasangani*
It	*Itivuttaka*
J	*Jataka*
KS	*Kindred Sayings*
Kvu	*Kathavatthu*
M	*Majjhima Nikaya*
Miln	*Milinda-panha*
Nett	*Netti-pakarana*
S	*Sanyutta Nikaya*
Sn	*Sutta-nipata*
Th 1	*Theragatha*
Th 2	*Therigatha*
Ud	*Udana*
Vbh	*Vibhanga*
Vin	*Vinaya*
Vism	*Visuddhi-magga*

Subject Index

Subject Index

Subject Index

Subject Index

Subject Index

Subject Index

Subject Index

Subject Index

Subject Index

Subject Index

Subject Index

Subject Index

Subject Index

Subject Index

Subject Index

Subject Index

Subject Index

Subject Index

FOOD
FOR THE THINKING
MIND

Throughout the history of mankind, serious thinkers in various parts of the world viewed our human existence and sought to find some meaning in it. They expressed their thoughts in wise sayings that have been preserved and have come down to us. This book is a collection of some of these sayings and is offered here so that we too may ponder on the meaning of our existence and come to understand some of our problems. These thoughts represent the wisdom of many sages and great thinkers. The aim is to draw attention to our common humanity and to show how similar we are to other members of the human race with regard to our joys, sorrows and our aspirations.

DEDICATION

With bad advisors forever left behind,
From paths of evil he departs for eternity,
Soon to see the Buddha of Limitless Light
And perfect Samantabhadra's Supreme Vows.

The supreme and endless blessings
of Samantabhadra's deeds,
I now universally transfer.
May every living being, drowning and adrift,
Soon return to the Land of
Limitless Light!

I vow that when my life approaches its end,
All obstructions will be swept away;
I will see Amitabha Buddha,
And be born in his Land of Ultimate Bliss and Peace.

When reborn in the Western Land,
I will perfect and completely fulfill
Without exception these Great Vows,
To delight and benefit all beings.

~ The Vows of Samantabhadra
Avatamsaka Sutra ~

NAME OF SPONSOR

助印功德芳名

Document Serial No：100337

委印文號：100337

Book Title: FOOD FOR THE THINKING MIND

Book Serial No.,書號：EN110

N.T.Dollars：

111,000：AMITABHA BUDDHIST SOCIETY OF U.S.A.

Total:N.T.Dollars 111,000；3,000 copies.

以上合計:新台幣 111,000 元；恭印 3,000 冊。

Place to contact and order in North America：

AMITABHA BUDDHIST SOCIETY OF U.S.A.

650 S. BERNARDO AVE, SUNNYVALE, CA 94087, U.S.A.

TEL:408-736-3386 FAX:408-736-3389

http://www.amtb-usa.org

DEDICATION OF MERIT

May the merit and virtue
accrued from this work
adorn Amitabha Buddha's Pure Land,
repay the four great kindnesses above,
and relieve the suffering of
those on the three paths below.

May those who see or hear of these efforts
generate Bodhi-mind,
spend their lives devoted to the Buddha Dharma,
and finally be reborn together in
the Land of Ultimate Bliss.
Homage to Amita Buddha!

NAMO AMITABHA
南無阿彌陀佛

財團法人佛陀教育基金會 印贈
台北市杭州南路一段五十五號十一樓
Printed and donated for free distribution by
The Corporate Body of the Buddha Educational Foundation
11F., 55 Hang Chow South Road Sec 1, Taipei, Taiwan, R.O.C.
Tel: 886-2-23951198 , Fax: 886-2-23913415
Email: overseas@budaedu.org
Website:http://www.budaedu.org

Printed in Taiwan
3,000 copies; October 2011
EN110-9705